SIMPLIFY

26 Simple Habits of Highly Successful People

DR. SHAH FAISAL AHMAD

CONTENTS

Introduction	vii
1. ATTRACTING SUCCESS through creative visualization	1
2. BELIEVE in yourself	2
3. COMMUNICATION skills	3
4. DECISIVENESS with clarity of mind and purpose	4
5. EFFICIENTLY manage the time	5
6. FOLLOWING one's bliss	7
7. GRATITUDE and giving	8
8. Watchful over which HABITS are being formed	9
9. Being IN CHARGE of one's own life	10
10. Jovial	11
11. KNOWLEDGEABLE, innovative and creative	12
12. LEADERSHIP and team-work	13
13. power of MOTIVATING others	14
14. NEGATING the fear	15
15. Optimism	16
16. Patience, Perseverance & Persistence	17
17. Quick-Witted	18
18. Resilience	19
19. Smart-Hard-Work	20
20. TAKING RISKS but smartly	21
21. Unselfconscious	22
22. Valiant	23
23. Will Power	24
24. Xcellence	25
25. Having a YOUTHFUL mind at every age	26
26. Zealous	27
27. ATTRACTING SUCCESS through creative visualization	28
28. BELIEVE in yourself	34
29. COMMUNICATION skills	40

30. DECISIVENESS with clarity of mind and purpose   44
31. EFFICIENTLY manage the time   51
32. FOLLOWING one's bliss   64
33. GRATITUDE and giving   69
34. Watchful over which HABITS are being formed   73
35. Being IN CHARGE of one's own life   76
36. Jovial   81
37. KNOWLEDGEABLE, innovative and creative   86
38. LEADERSHIP and team-work   92
39. power of MOTIVATING others   100
40. NEGATING the fear   103
41. Optimism   105
42. Patience, Perseverance & Persistence   108
43. Quick-Witted   116
44. Resilience   119
45. Smart-Hard-Work   122
46. TAKING RISKS but smartly   125
47. Unselfconscious   127
48. Valiant   129
49. Will Power   132
50. Xcellence   135
51. Having a YOUTHFUL mind at every age   138
52. Zealous   141

Afterword   145

We are dedicating this book to you, the reader, if you are the one who believes in achieving your highest potential and in following your bliss.

INTRODUCTION

Why is it that very few people have been fully successful in living the kind of life they want but not others? Why is it that that most of us claim just "luck" to be the deciding factor of our destinies when we have been bestowed with the two hands, two feet, one brain and the "freewill"? What immerses some humans in their dreams so much so that they start following them blindly, without knowing that they how they would reach there? What makes other people help them in following their dreams while at the same time killing their own dreams? Are you missing something from this short journey of your life on earth? What is it that separates you from your idols or the men/women who live the life the way you too want to live? Too many questions, one simple answer – The habituated qualities!

It seems that the majority of people are pretty lousy when it comes to understanding why people succeed or fail. They will give you an answer which is just one small piece of the puzzle - the high achievers are born predisposed to certain productive talents and lacking in those that cause failure. In fact, successful people are the ones who live their life the way they want to live. They reach their personal and professional goals not because of who they are but because of what their qualities or characteristics are which in turn develop into their habits or the things they do every time.

The first thing you would require, to get what you want in life, would be an unprecedented surge of motivation. You would waste your precious time looking here and there for the sake of getting motivated. What we have done is that, we have researched the top and common qualities of the super successful people in the world, mostly from the 20th and 21st century. We have also researched on their real life stories that are in harmony with these top qualities. We have arranged these 26 qualities in such a way that they correspond to the 26 letters of the alphabet, so that it becomes easier for you to memorize them. Each time you would read a story, you would start getting boosted up. You would simultaneously like to acquire those qualities into your life, and make them your habits. The short and to the point details of each quality are also provided in each chapter for this purpose.

While you are reading about these qualities, listen to the words in your heart as well as in your mind. Slow down and let each quality feel like your own for the time being. Imagine what it would be like if that characteristic trait was already yours and then work towards acquiring that quality in your life. Just dreaming about being the person you want to be won't take you there. You have to see what makes them different from you. You have to see what makes them do those things differently which, to your surprise, you too might be doing almost daily. Then you have to analyse what thing stops you from acquiring that quality if you ever tried it. Remove that impediment and see the magic. Let your inner-self have a personal relationship with each quality while you are reading about it.

Neither we are having any personal liking for the people

mentioned in this book, nor do you need to have. The real motto behind writing this book is to make it clear that the humans are so smart creatures that their highest potentials are locked in the process of possessing and using these 26 qualities (or may be a few more). The people mentioned in this book have unlocked their respective highest human potentials and it is the need of the hour to spread those stories, and the qualities associated with them, to every person living on this planet now and to those who will be born in the near future (our kids). We can make ourselves achieve whatever our minds perceive, just by having a little bit of discipline in acquiring and/or enhancing these qualities. Then, the excellence and perfection that would embrace our world would be worth watching.

Chapter One

ATTRACTING SUCCESS THROUGH CREATIVE VISUALIZATION

The ultimate power of Creative visualization
 The magic wand of the subconscious mind
 Programming the reticular activating system (RAS)
 The law of attraction
 The two richest Americans
 They wanted it to happen, visualized it happening and it happened
 Visualize what you want to be and you will be
 You can use it anywhere, at anytime
 Creative visualization makes the rags to riches stories
 Can we achieve anything we want through visualization?

Chapter Two
BELIEVE IN YOURSELF

The force that pushes us and the one that pulls us
    The wish that remains a wish
    Let them criticize
    Keep your money and let me keep my self-belief
    You are not a failure unless you believe you are
    Taking a giant leap forward
    Failing even 200 times is not a big deal till you believe you can
    The women who believed in themselves

Chapter Three

COMMUNICATION SKILLS

One can always learn how to communicate in a better way
    Loading dose and maintenance dose
    The "One more thing"
    Good boss and Great boss
    Communication in a comprehendible manner
    The communication tactics of Branson
    Picking up the phone

Chapter Four

DECISIVENESS WITH CLARITY OF MIND AND PURPOSE

Clarity of Mind
    A clear mind is like a calm lake
    Clarity of purpose
    How to achieve clarity of purpose
    Decisiveness
    Decide quickly and firmly but change it slowly
    Make lists and live by them
    Focus and decision making go hand in hand
    Decision taken, goal visualized but these obstacles!
    There would have been no Harry Potter without decisiveness
    Destiny is shaped in your moments of decision
    Set big goals and believe they would come true

Chapter Five
EFFICIENTLY MANAGE THE TIME

Can we actually manage the "time"?
    Why to manage our time?
    Do they have more than 24 hours in day?
    Have a vision or go just waste your time
    Write them down and review your plans
    Checklist for every task
    The amazing powers of cushion-time
    How successful people make use of cushion time?
    <u>1. Aiming secretly and finishing genuinely</u>
    <u>2. Lengthening the total duration by adding cushions</u>
    <u>3. Using the Slack Time</u>
    <u>4. The task contingencies</u>
    <u>5. Time cushions as buffers</u>
    Plan, sleep, wake up and execute
    The question to be asked to yourself
    Don't delay it, Delegate it
    Where to and where not to multitask
    Where to and where not to procrastinate
    Chunk it down
    Blocks of time

- Energy management
- Balance
- Be organized
- Avoiding interruptions
- Bunch those bananas up
- Waking up early in the morning

Chapter Six

FOLLOWING ONE'S BLISS

1. Living your dream makes your life worth living.

2. You can be a source of inspiration to others.

3. You'll meet other dream seekers.

4. When you work on something you don't like, your whole life would be hell.

5. The internal happiness that comes along with the process of following one's dreams is the eternal one.

6. The best thing about dreams is that they are like fingerprints.

7. You can prove all those people wrong that stopped you from following your dream.

8. Following your bliss will make yourself and your family proud.

9. Surely the life is short and you live only once.

Chapter Seven

GRATITUDE AND GIVING

Filling a bucket with a hole at bottom
- The heavenly feeling of gratitude
- The power of giving
- The more we celebrate, the more there is to celebrate
- Serving others is the secret
- Trading expectation for appreciation

Chapter Eight

WATCHFUL OVER WHICH HABITS ARE BEING FORMED

Leave the actions that can become obstacles
    Acquiring the habits that take you towards the dreams
    The qualities that you admire the most
    Chains which are too heavy to be broken
    Qualities mentioned in this book

Chapter Nine

BEING IN CHARGE OF ONE'S OWN LIFE

Everyone knows it, No one applies it
- Rejecting the path of least resistance
- Being responsible for one's own failure
- The blame game
- Stop blaming and start steering
- You – the master of your fate, the captain of your soul
- Control your attitude and master the change
- Use the pain and pleasure instead of having them use you
- The person who knows how to bend the Universe
- Be responsible for becoming proactive and productive

Chapter Ten
JOVIAL

The more jovial you are the more likeable you would be
    Being jovial allows for bonding
    Being cheerful relieves that load of stress
    The cheerful guy is always invited.
    The great networking tool
    A good sense of humor facilitates trust.
    Being jovial increases group effectiveness and productivity
    Jovial people are more outgoing.

Chapter Eleven

KNOWLEDGEABLE, INNOVATIVE AND CREATIVE

The golden sword of knowledge
    Those who innovate
    The power of creativity
    Education gives you an edge
    Innovate on a constant basis
    Think but smartly
    Never hesitate to steal great ideas
    Think out of the box
    Imitate but uniquely
    Being experienced matters
    The Emotional Intelligence
    Imagination is better than knowledge

Chapter Twelve

LEADERSHIP AND TEAM-WORK

They have a great deal of Self Control
- Successful leaders have courageous hearts
- Definiteness of Decisions, and making high quality ones
- Detail oriented and effective communication
- Better sense of Judgment
- Understanding and empathy
- Skilful Planning
- Responsibility and accountability
- A trusted leader, not just a leader
- Good personality, positive attitude & being powerfully passionate
- Team work
- Humility
- Sense of Humor
- Commitment
- Creativity and Intuition
- A deep search for talent
- Empowering others

Chapter Thirteen
POWER OF MOTIVATING OTHERS

The Reality Distortion Field
    The first part of this definition
    The second part of this definition
    Motivate them and get momentum
    .

Chapter Fourteen

NEGATING THE FEAR

The power lies within your beliefs

Handling your failure

The two powerful ways – follow the first, modify the second

Chapter Fifteen
OPTIMISM

A dollar bill on the ground
    Wisdom of early 20th century
    Attitude to climb matters, altitude of mountain doesn't
    Why are we right the either way according to Ford?

Chapter Sixteen

PATIENCE, PERSEVERANCE & PERSISTENCE

Three P's of Rockefeller
    The vision for future
    Willing to go the extra mile
    Nothing can take place of persistence
    Drive, determination and persistence
    The mindset of Buffett
    The dresses made out of potato sacks
    His pursuit of Happiness
    Women aren't weak for having persistence

Chapter Seventeen
QUICK-WITTED

The farsighted quick-witted Gates
    The Rich neighbour and the 2 thieves
    Just show up and be quick-witted
    If you are experienced, trust your instincts and take quick action
    It is far better if you can play with numbers too

Chapter Eighteen
RESILIENCE

Resilience pushes you forward
    Welcome the criticism
    The women power
    The survival of the fittest

Chapter Nineteen
SMART-HARD-WORK

The power of intelligence
    Be smart in innovation as well
    Smartness in delegation
    You don't need to be Einstein or Arnold
    Be smart or go home

Chapter Twenty

TAKING RISKS BUT SMARTLY

Highly productive, easily reversible
    Prediction and far-sightedness
    Protecting the downside
    The greatest risk in life

Chapter Twenty-One
UNSELFCONSCIOUS

I don't care
    I have other important decisions to make
    That grey t-shirt on every occasion
    First get to that level and then think about the edge

Chapter Twenty-Two
VALIANT

The real problem
    Big problems as just a bunch of little problems
    Play life like a videogame
    The difference lies in perception
    Learning lessons from failure

Chapter Twenty-Three
WILL POWER

Will power fights dyslexia
    Don't worry if they call you an obstinate
    I want it and I will have it
    I can and I will

Chapter Twenty-Four
XCELLENCE

Excellence is cultivable
    Excellence in earning money
    Excellence in his own work
    Excellence in managing time
    Major in major things

Chapter Twenty-Five

HAVING A YOUTHFUL MIND AT EVERY AGE

The secret code of Steve Jobs
    The part of his game
    Never give 100% perfect review
    Never settle down as you are not mud

Chapter Twenty-Six
ZEALOUS

He sold ties to his classmates and they still buy them from him

Passion has energy

Focus brings enthusiasm

Be results-focussed rather than activity-focussed

He doesn't stop writing and thus remains zealous and famous

Chapter Twenty-Seven

ATTRACTING SUCCESS THROUGH CREATIVE VISUALIZATION

You become what you think about most. But you also attract what you think about most - John Assaraf

Visualization is the wonderful process of imagining vivid pictures or the act of visualizing any scenario in our mind's eye. We do it every day and almost every time, even during our sleep when we are submerged in the ocean of dreams. However, there are people who claim that their brains are so "dumb" that they don't see anything in their imaginations. Although if we ask them to recall anything exciting or hilarious that happened years before, they would even be able to draw a good picture of the scene on paper. So, we can just call it mental laziness of not putting enough effort to imagine anything while reading, listening or thinking.

On the other hand, there are people, living on this planet, alongside the self-claimed dumb minds, who have turned the tables over and over again, going from rags to riches, from being zeroes to heroes, from being mediocre to champions, only through the process of creative visualization.

. . .

The ultimate power of Creative visualization

It is a miraculous technique in which we can use our imagination to create and visualize the scenarios in our mind's eye. We can create the mental picture of anything we want and then keep focussing on this scenario or image for periods of time on a daily basis. The main idea behind creative visualization is that when we change our thoughts and perceptions which are holding us back, we can change our current status of life. We can improvise ourselves to bring our desires to us more quickly.

The magic wand of the subconscious mind

The process of creative visualization activates the creative powers of our subconscious mind. Our mind has been bestowed with a power which lets us transmute our desires into their physical equivalents. You might have observed the kick that you get when you are extremely hungry and someone describes the taste and experience of eating some new variety of pizza in market or some dish which has been your favourite delicacy. Your mouth starts watering with just the visuals of you eating this dish. You can't help yourself picking up the phone and calling the pizza delivery shop or getting up and going to the restaurant to fulfil your appetite with the same dish you just visualized. Your fire of hunger would have been extinguished with even a stale loaf of bread sitting just next to you, but what made that bread piece envy your favourite dish was not your food favouritism, but the strong mental imagery of you eating the dish, that activated your subconscious mind. This in turn drove the wheels of your physical body to get off your butt, take action and create what you desired. Same thing happens when we use the creative visualization for our goals.

. . .

Programming the reticular activating system (RAS)

The creative visualization programmes our brain's reticular activating system (RAS) in order to make it capable of noticing the previously unnoticed "available resources" that were always there. The day you make up your mind to shop for clothes in the evening, you might have observed that at least once on that day, you kept noticing how other people look in the type of garments you want to buy. You never did the same thing any other day, did you?

The successful people do the same thing for achieving their desires and ambitions. When they activate their mind through creative visualization of what they want, they now become capable of noticing the opportunities that used to be there all the time but just were not noticeable.

The law of attraction

Creative visualization magnetizes to us the people, the opportunities and the resources that we need to achieve our goals. It works through the famous "law of attraction" according to which we attract into our lives those things and situations which we keep constantly thinking and imagining about, using our deepest emotions.

The two richest Americans

Bill Gates, the richest American and the chairman of Microsoft, had visualized the computers running on every desk and Microsoft software on every computer long before it ever happened. **John D Rockefeller** became the world's first billionaire and is still counted as the America's richest person in history. He went from rags to riches only through the process of creative visualization combined with his awesome quality of perseverance, which he used to often brag about.

They wanted it to happen, visualized it happening and it happened

It was **Henry Ford** who imagined a car in every driveway before it turned out to be a reality. **Steve jobs** developed a vision for Apple in his mind to develop the products with elegant design and simple user interface that would please all age groups and that is what an established reality is today. **Mark Zuckerberg** visualized a more open and connected world and he has succeeded in connecting people all over the planet and building a more empathetic world.

Visualize what you want to be and you will be

Michael Jordan, the all time famous basketball champion, visualized where he wanted to be and what kind of player he wanted to become. He knew exactly where he wanted to go and just focused on getting there. **Arnold Schwarzenegger** said that long before he won his first Mr. Universe title, he used to walk around the tournament like he owned it. He had won it so many times in his mind that he believed with full conviction that he already owned that title. He used the power of attracting success through creative visualization again when he moved into the field of movies. He daily visualized being a successful actor and earning lots and lots of money and today we all know where he stands. "It's all in the mind", says Arnold.

You can use it anywhere, at anytime

Tiger Woods claims to have been using creative visualization techniques for attracting success from a very early age. He has been using the incredible power of his mind to visualize exactly where he wants his golf ball to stop. Today, he is one of the famous and successful golf players all over the world. Top Olympic athletes and other great sportsmen simulate the game in their heads and visualize themselves as the winner and a star performer a day before they actually play it.

It has been studied that if the sportsmen are trained in their minds about the tips and tricks of their game, they perform with equal results (or sometimes better) than the sportsmen who train for equal time actually on the ground. It is because our mind cannot distinguish between something which has been visualized over and over again in the mental imagery and something that happened in reality.

Creative visualization makes the rags to riches stories

Jim Carrey is one of those rags to riches guy. In 1987, he wrote a check to himself for 10 million US dollars and dated it for Thanksgiving 1995, and also added a note "for services rendered." After visualizing on this for years, he received exactly 10 million dollars for his role in *Dumb and Dumber* in 1994. **Oprah Winfrey**, who arose to become one of the most powerful women in the world, openly advocates the use of creative visualization techniques. She talks about the affirmations, power of the subconscious mind and other goal focusing techniques regularly on her talk show. Not only this, she also makes her own vision boards in order to strengthen the process of visualization.

Can we achieve anything we want through visualization?

As mentioned before, the whole idea here is that our

brains are unable to discriminate between what has been imagined on a constant basis or with extreme vividness, and what is the reality. This is why our dreams appear so real at times that it takes us a couple of minutes in the morning to see if we are awake now, or to know where the hell we are now!

This inability of our brains has served us as a boon for creating and attracting the lives we want. Many quantum physicists and psychologists agree that our strongly emotionalized thoughts which we keep thinking or images which we keep visualizing, on a constant basis, keep generating energetic waves that attract the objects, opportunities or resources for our goals that we want in our lives. According to them, each clear emotionalized thought has a frequency and the power to attract things.

Putting it simply, if we have a very clear picture of what we want, we are more likely to find the path that is necessary to get us there where we want to be than if we don't really know what we want. We define our target this way, as opposed to not knowing where our target is.

The law of attraction works every time for every person, even if we believe in it or not. It is a law of nature just like any other law. The law of gravity is a law of nature that doesn't care who you are and if you fall from the rooftop of your home, you are going to break your bones, in spite of your caste, creed, color, nature, age and sex. Similarly, the law of attraction is a law of nature and has been proved to be true by all the successful, influential and wealthy people who believed in it, harnessed the power of their imagination, visualized their success beforehand and became what they wanted to be.

Chapter Twenty-Eight
BELIEVE IN YOURSELF

Whether you think you can, or you think you can't - Either way you're right - Henry Ford

It is neither the intelligence nor the resources or opportunities that stand out as the biggest difference between successful people and unsuccessful people. However, it's all about believing in your own self that you can achieve your goals. If we start believing in ourselves, people will be forced to believe in us, whatever our goals or ambitions may be. Self-belief is probably the single most important trait possessed by any successful person that walked on the surface of earth. If we don't believe in ourselves, how come do we expect others to believe in us? You won't get too far, if you don't believe you can succeed.

The force that pushes us and the one that pulls us

It is all about being sure that you are going to do whatever you want even if others are against you. There is a positive motivational force all over the universe which we fail to recognize until we get clear on what we want to do and unless we believe that we can do it. However, with every seed of positivity, you will find weeds of negative forces arising out of every situation you face and out of almost every person to whom you reveal your big ambitions. They will, knowingly or unknowingly try to bring you down; because they are the ones who didn't "believe in themselves" that they could ever do that what you have made up your mind to do. How can they let you go for achieving your dreams, unless they belong to the category of that 1% of the people who inspire and help others in achieving their dreams (even if they failed at achieving theirs).

Under the pressure of this criticism, most of the people start to doubt their own abilities and then eventually give up. There are only a few people, who manage to give a deaf ear to what others are saying about their dreams, who only keep listening to what their strong hearts have to say. These are the people who believe in themselves. They continue moving along the path they've chosen and simply are the ones who succeed and create history.

The wish that remains a wish

Millions of people fail to live the life they have always wished to live. Their "wish" always remained a "wish". As soon as they encounter the first obstacle, they give up on their big dreams and fail to realize their ambitions. One of the strongest causes for this attitude is that they do not believe in themselves.

Well you have not bought this book to discuss the attitude of failures, did u? So, let us not lose heart by knowing why the failures failed. That actually feels like listening to a sad song when your heart breaks and becoming sadder. Let us jump straightaway on to knowing the people who believed in themselves and did what their hearts said. They were just like everyone else, with same eyes, ears, nose, tongue, brains and organs stuffed in their bodies. They just used to hold their ambitions strongly in their mental imagery all the time and believed that they could do it, even if no one else did that before. They did it and turned the milk of their "wish" into the delicious cheese of "reality".

Let them criticize

Warren Buffet's success comes mostly from his refusal to follow the crowd and his ability to believe in his own skills. With his unique stock-picking skills, this self-made billionaire is regarded as one of the most brilliant investors today. Every Tom, Dick and Harry was buying internet stocks madly during the Dot Com boom of 1990's. Among the few entrepreneurs who didn't buy these stocks was Warren Buffet and he was highly criticized for his skepticism and extreme caution when dealing with these new stocks. Few years later, after the Dot Com crash happened, everyone lost huge amounts of money while Warren Buffet ended up being the second richest man in the world.

Keep your money and let me keep my self-belief

Mark Zuckerberg was offered close to $10 million dollars for the website by an investor when his brainchild Facebook was just four months old. The offer was tempting, but he declined and stuck with his baby. Other failed attempts were made by Google, Viacom, News Corp. at convincing Zuckerberg that he cannot handle this social networking site and he should quit handling it and sell it to these big guns of that time. Then, Yahoo came by in 2006 and offered a cool $1 billion cheque to Zuckerberg as they felt millions were just not good enough for him to sell it. But

Zuckerberg stuck with his baby and kept believing in himself in spite of knowing the risks he would probably have to face if another strong competitor for his social networking site arose out of somewhere. While he was feeling grateful for watching its rise in popularity, Microsoft came knocking at his door in 2007 with a $15 billion offer. Zuckerberg believed in his product as well as in his vision and rejected this offer as well even though these were still the early days for Facebook. And then just a few years later, the $15 billion seemed to everyone like a poor man's play as the gush and rush of Facebook conquered the world.

You are not a failure unless you believe you are

Let's talk about the multi-million dollar company, Apple founder **Steve Jobs**. Do you know that he was kicked out of his own company by the board over his own personal visions and how he was running the company? It clearly sounds discouraging and cruel, but not for Steve Jobs. Jobs believed in his vision and knew that he was going to continue believing and acting towards what he liked to do. After he got kicked out, he ended up starting a new startup computer company - NeXT which developed a next generation operating system, arose to become the CEO of Pixar, which turned small animations studio into a global animation organization with massive fame and eventually redeemed control of Apple. The people, who believe in themselves and their vision, don't care about being knocked down or getting failed. They know that they can rise from zero again due to their mastery of the process of achieving. He took his failure of getting kicked out of his own company in a positive way helping him to gain more experience at other companies. He made Apple one of the greatest companies of all time and his own story of self-belief a history.

. . .

Taking a giant leap forward

The creation of Amazon by **Jeff Bezos** was the result of a leap of faith. Jeff not only left a comfortable Wall Street career, but he also thought of entering a world he knew little about. The only thing he knew was that the idea of creating Amazon was "so obvious and compelling" that he had to leap. He believed that he could start it, make it one of the leading internet websites and he did it.

Failing even 200 times is not a big deal till you believe you can

If you fail 10 times, and you are a determined person, you will stand up the 11th time. But if you get failed 100th time, would you still continue believing in yourself or any product of your creativity? Now double this number of failure or rejections, would you still be alive? **Alex Haley**, the world famous best-selling author, received 200 rejections before he published the novel "Roots". It was his unshakable belief in his creativity that not only was his novel got published in 37 languages but he also won the Pulitzer Prize for the same. This novel also became a popular television miniseries in 1977.

The women who believed in themselves

You don't need to be a man of good luck, or born with a golden spoon in your mouth to be an ardent believer in yourself. **JK Rowling** claimed that rock bottom was the solid foundation on which she rebuilt her life. She had a short lived marriage, was a jobless alone parent and homeless at one time (and of course having clinical depression, who wouldn't have it in such conditions). Yet, she believed in her writings, she knew her words had power, her imaginations had an impact and continued writing novels and who doesn't know the grand success of her "Harry Potter series" of novels. According to Rowling, we do not need magic to transform our world. All the power we need is already inside ourselves. There is yet another woman who believed in herself, believed that she was destined for greatness and believed that she would be successful - **Oprah Winfrey**. Oprah strongly believes that we don't become what we just "want" or simply "wish" to be, we become what we "believe we can be". She believed that she would be a success, and there she is.

These examples were not of people who lived on other planets. They were/are just normal people like you; they just had the last laugh because they believed in themselves. If you don't believe in yourself you will eventually end up discarding your great ideas. You would be like other normal people who have breakfast, lunch and dinner, go to sleep, poop a lot and work underpaid from 9-5, while thinking all the time about the great life you would have been living only if you had believed in yourself and your dreams. Only if!

Chapter Twenty-Nine
COMMUNICATION SKILLS

To effectively communicate, we must realize that we are all different in the way we perceive the world and use this understanding as a guide to our communication with others - Tony Robbins

When you are trying to move ahead in life in terms of your employment, business, and personal relationships or with regards to your community, one of the most important things that you would need to consider is having or developing the skill of effective communication. You will find that without this skill, things will quickly turn into chaos. You may be perceiving the best and the most brilliant ideas in your skull, but if you can't vent them out effectively, they may have to be thrown into the garbage box. Effective communication involves both speaking and listening efficiently (and in today's world emailing and chatting efficiently). Developing this as a characteristic trait turns small salesperson into giant entrepreneurs, employees into employers and mediocre persons into respectable socialites.

. . .

One can always learn how to communicate in a better way

One thing is sure about effective communication skills that some people are born with them and some aren't, but other thing which is sure about them is that almost anyone can learn them and at any age. Effective communication is something that can be easily taught. People who make the effort to learn this important skill always come out profited from the experience. It helps both in terms of your personal life and your work. In fact communicating clearly will make your life a great deal easier.

Loading dose and maintenance dose

The first change that occurs in people who make up their minds to be successful is in the way they talk and behave. They start acting as if they already have got what they aspire for. This is the loading dose of the new attitude that they have to maintain later on when they achieve it. When they achieve what they want, their new and improved way of communication becomes their character. Same is true with those who were born great, except that their loading dose of communication skills starts right from the time they are taught how to speak.

The "One more thing"

The best entrepreneurs know how to sell their products by effective communication. **Steve Jobs** regularly saved the best for last part his speech when launching new products. After having unveiled a raft of new gadgets, just as the audience used to be ready to leave, Jobs would utter the words "One more thing..." There was always a mischievous smile when he did so. It was, no doubt, a part of his genius as a showman. These "One more things" have included the iPod touch, Powerbook G4, and Facetime video calling.

Good boss and Great boss

As they say that a good boss follows his instincts but a great boss listens to his employees, same is true of **Mark Zuckerberg**. Back in 2005, when Mark Zuckerberg was busy in meetings with the venture capitalists for Facebook, he used to disappear for long stretches of time. This way, he used to leave his employees with no vision for the future and literally no plan to work according to.

A senior executive informed Zuckerberg that he has a lack of CEO-like behaviour and that his employees are losing motivation day by day due to the same. This may have been so because of the early (seemingly not so mature) age at which he joined entrepreneurship. However, Zuckerberg listened, found the mentors for helping him to improve his communication skills and now, he's a professional CEO. The current employees of Facebook are said to applaud him as he gives them a clear picture of where the company is and where it is going.

Communication in a comprehendible manner

Warren Buffet always simplifies the technical details so that it becomes easier for all his shareholders to understand the business in which they have invested. This is a sure sign that he really understands his own businesses. He believes in communicating well with each and every person who is important to his business.

The communication tactics of Branson

Richard Branson believes that at a certain workplace, the boss and his or her employees should communicate so well that it should seem that they are working together towards the same goal. He believes that if all the employees are not using "we" to associate themselves with the company, it is a sign that people who are up and down the chain of command aren't communicating.

Branson also says that you must learn to be a good listener in order to succeed. Seeking a number of opinions in business from a variety of experienced people "can save you a lot of time and money," says Branson. He suggests that we should not tell people about others' suggestions until we've heard what they have to say. This is because in the end, maybe we decide that the best advice is to walk away—and later we find out it was the only best solution.

Picking up the phone

In this era of new gadgets, it is always cool to be tech-savvy. However, you should not text or email when you should be calling. **Richard Branson** believes that the quality of business communications has started to become poorer in recent years. This is because people avoid phone calls and face-to-face meetings. He believes that solving long disputes over emailing can be inefficient and lead to more disputes. The best way of course is to have face to face communication or if distance prevents so, calling over the phone restores that power of human connection which solves any damn issue or brings forth better opportunities than texting or emailing.

Chapter Thirty

DECISIVENESS WITH CLARITY OF MIND AND PURPOSE

In any moment of decision, the best thing you can do is the right thing. The worst thing you can do is nothing – Theodore Roosevelt

Clarity of Mind

Clarity of mind refers to the mental state of being free from any doubtful questions, no more noise in your head, no more confused thoughts and no more prejudices inside your skull. While some exceptional people are always able to maintain their clarity of mind, some attain it in difficult situations by calming their mind like a calm lake. It is the faith, the silence, the process of letting go, the forgiving, and the focus on deep breathing (or on meditation) that work wonders in achieving mental clarity when in stress.

A clear mind is like a calm lake

When even a tiny pebble is dropped on a calm lake, gentle but energetic ripples start out there. Similarly when our mind is clear, it responds by generating fresh thoughts and ideas providing a solution to our problems. In contrast, our restless mind is similar to a glass full of mud and water which stirs more and more with the spoon of stress. We need to allow the mud to settle down and then the water becomes clear. This is how muddy thinking can be replaced by clear thinking. Successful people always are clear regarding the thoughts they have in mind and clear on the purpose they give to themselves. So, let's talk about another trait of successful people of having "Clarity of purpose".

Clarity of purpose

According to **Napoleon Hill**, the author of the international bestseller "Think and grow rich", There is one quality that one must possess to win, and that is definiteness of purpose, the knowledge of what one wants, and a burning desire to possess it. So, our dream should not just be a wish. It must be transformed into specific and clear goals. When you get clarity of purpose, you just automatically get to know what steps you will have to take in order to achieve the goal. Clarity of purpose is like focusing an intense beam of light on your goal, so that you are able to see it clearly.

How to achieve clarity of purpose

Many life coaches and mentors suggest that we should write down both the short term and long term goals on a piece of paper with a clear plan of how to achieve each goal, what you intend to give in return of the goal getting accomplished and the time limit for achieving the goal. This paper should be read twice daily until you can see and believe clearly that your goal is surely attainable. The image of your goal should be so emotionalized and fixed so well in the mind that every time you read that paper, you get boosted up. This is what most of the successful people do. **W. Clement Stone**, one of the richest persons of America learnt it from Napoleon Hill. **Jack Canfield**, the bestselling author and self made millionaire learnt about this clarity of purpose from W. Clement Stone and is a live example of how being clear on our purpose can fetch us the results we want.

Decisiveness

Decisiveness refers to having the power or quality of deciding something after putting an end to all sorts of controversy in the mind and be determined and definite about what needs to be done.

A core quality in a successful person is "being decisive" and then be able to take suitable action. When decisions need to be made, the successful people gather the facts, analyze the situation, consider alternatives, and plan the best course of action and they do it quickly. They move and take action. Failures may also decide strongly and clearly, but they procrastinate, and stand around wringing their hands. Once a decision is made, there should be no looking back because even the best decision can be undermined if there is lack of support and some backroom second guessing.

Decide quickly and firmly but change it slowly

Decisive people keep in mind the need for modifications. They understand that their decisions may not be perfect and never hesitate to modify or alter their decisions when the original decision clearly doesn't seem to be working out exactly as planned. So, you may ask what the fun of taking that first, not so fruitful decision was. The successful people know that taking no action at all and wasting time on thinking only is far worse than making a decision and taking action even if it needs to be changed later on. Further, being flexible is awesome, but you should follow **Henry Ford**'s formula here: Be quick to take the decision with faith and be slow and thoughtful in changing it later if needed. Most of the people do the reverse and that is why they are not the owners of Ford Motor Company.

Make lists and live by them

Richard Branson focuses on staying organized and keeping lists: lists of people to call, lists of ideas, lists of companies to set up, lists of people who can make things happen. He works each day through these lists, and this thing propels him forward. Of course, the listing of things to be done is important because it gives a sense of clarity and we already are aware by now that how important the clarity of mind is.

Focus and decision making go hand in hand

Henry Ford used to say that there is no man living who isn't capable of doing more than he thinks he can. We, as humans, rule the earth, but are still completely unaware of our potential. Well some of us do know about our potential and try to achieve the height we can reach before we expire. However, most of the people never bother to know how much we can accomplish. This is because of two reasons

1. They don't know how to reach their highest potential and stick with the sentence, "we will make less, eat less and thus, won't be tense"

2. They've never focused all of their efforts on one task at a time. Recent research has proved that human brains are not

designed for multitasking and if we try to do so, our efficiency of doing each of those tasks decreases.

When you focus our life and take decisions with clarity of mind and purpose, impossibilities become possibilities. So, get focused and you can do more than you (currently) think you can.

Decision taken, goal visualized but these obstacles!

Ever witnessed a waterfall? When water reaches the top of waterfall from its source, it has that gravity in it; it knows that where it has to go with this gravity and it has of course made its mind to do so. Now, there are big rocks along its path, the obstacles! Have you ever seen water fearing that it might not cross those obstacles and thus, going back against gravity towards its source? Well, surely that is absurd and never happens. Let us see what happens instead. The water first tries to move downwards over those rocks and then, reaches the bottom of the fall. It then gets that momentum and starts making its own ways through the crevices and spaces between the rocks. Then finally when it gains more momentum, it moulds those rocks, slices them off and clears its path for an eternal and magnificent flow that attracts people from all over the world.

Suppose the gravity disappears all of a sudden. What will happen? Does the water on the top of the waterfall now know where to go? What would be its goal? Would it still have the same impact on those rocks? No, something happened and this water had to take its eyes off the goal. So, obstacles are only those frightful things that we experience only when we take our eyes off the goal. It is the goal that motivates and gives you the strength to keep moving forward. You must consistently see the goal as complete and experience the goal as if already accomplished in your imagination.

There would have been no Harry Potter without decisiveness

How many of you get superb ideas about writing a novel, a book, a script for a movie? Almost all. How many of you turn that idea into a decision? Almost none. **JK Rowling** would have been the same as ordinary people. She got that idea for Harry very clearly in mind but just out of nowhere. You might also daydream out of nowhere about fairytales and superheroes (depending on your sex) almost all the time, don't you? The next thing that she made to happen was what separates her from others. She took a firm decision of writing a whole novel series about Harry Potter and she was so clear about her decision that she outlined the plots for each book and started writing her first novel *Harry Potter and the Sorcerer's Stone,* and there she is today, one of the best author and richest women of the world. She proved that all it takes is one good idea and a perfect sense of decisiveness to reach there where one can only be in their dreams when caught up in the cage of indecision.

Destiny is shaped in your moments of decision

Tony Robbins, one of the richest motivational speakers and authors, very clearly believes that our destiny gets shaped only in those moments in which we take the decision.

Set big goals and believe they would come true

John D Rockefeller used to set out huge goals. When he was a young boy, he set out two life-long goals:

1. To make one million big ones,
2. To live up to 100 years of age

Although he carved his name in gold in the books of history regarding his first goal by being the richest American who ever lived, he died 3 years short of his second goal, 97 years old. He proved to us that our brain is a goal seeking organism and we can accomplish anything we want by just deciding what we want and visualizing it clearly.

Chapter Thirty-One
EFFICIENTLY MANAGE THE TIME

Dost thou love life? Then do not squander time, for that's the stuff that life is made of - Benjamin Franklin

Time management refers to the process of organizing and planning how long you spend on specific activities. The people who are able to manage their time exceptionally well are the highest achievers. By using the efficient time-management techniques mentioned in this chapter, that have been used by all the highest achievers of the past and present, you can improve your ability to function more effectively and productively – even when pressures are high and the time is tight. **Jim Rohn**, an American entrepreneur, author, a motivational speaker whose rags to riches story is famous, referred time management as "the best-kept secret of the rich". However, here in this chapter, all secrets of effective time management are revealed for you.

Can we actually manage the "time"?

According **Bob Proctor**, the motivational author, business consultant, entrepreneur, and a teacher who preaches the value of positive thinking, maximizing human potential and self-motivation, the time cannot be managed. Instead we can manage activities. Managing our activities begins with planning and it is so simple that there is not a trick to it. Each night, write out a list of what to do tomorrow. Wake up and do it. However, we have been using the term "time management" since a long time. So what time is it that we can manage? If you are thinking it is the clock time then you are wrong because that keeps on running and never listens to anyone. The time we can manage is the real time.

All time is relative in real time. The time drags or flies depending on what you are doing. If you spend two hours waiting outside a dentist's clinic with ghost of pain in your mouth, it can feel like 10 long years. And yet our 10-year-old kids seem to have grown up in only 2 hours. Nevertheless, this real time is all that exists in our mind and is manageable. You are the ones who create it and thus, you can manage it.

Why to manage our time?

If at all people come to know how managing their time in a better way would make them more productive they would start investing their whole time and money for acquiring good time management skills. However, people choose to go with the wind and just start working fast, hesitantly and make mistakes. It may seem counter-intuitive to dedicate your precious time in learning about the time management and how successful people manage their time, instead of using it to just blindly get on with your work. However, the benefits are enormous: You can become productive and efficient, you can get less stressed, your professional reputation would get increased and you would avail for yourself greater opportunities for advancement and achieving your career goals.

On the other hand, if you fail to manage your time effectively, there can be some very undesirable consequences: You are highly likely to miss your deadlines, your quality of work would be poor, the flow of your work would be inefficient, you would lament your poor professional reputation, your stress levels would be higher and you can't grab the opportunities that can help you in achieving your goals.

Do they have more than 24 hours in day?

Sometimes you get astonished at people who have the same level of education as you have, same skills that you have developed and, of course, the same amount of time in a day as you have - "the 24 hours" and yet they seem to be more productive than you are. On the other hand, it may also seem to you that there is never enough time in your day. However, since we all get the same 24 hours, why the difference and where are you lagging behind? The answer lies in efficient time management. Managing the time efficiently requires you to shift your focus from activities to results, from quantity of time spent in finishing a task to quality of effort in finishing the task, and from changing your mind frequently during the task to planning beforehand and sticking to it. So, it is all about working smarter, not harder so that you are able to get more done in less time.

Have a vision or go just waste your time

In case you are not having a perfectly clear and specific goal/project in your mind for which you are working, then there is no need of managing your time. As they say, if you don't know where you have to go, then any path would take you there and in fact any time would be specific for you to reach there. However, when you have a clear and specific goal/project in your mind and you are striving towards executing it "keeping the end in mind", you would yourself find a driving force or enthusiasm to take you there. Every successful person had a vision that took them there on or before exactly the same time they wished to reach there. Well that is what is called a goal: a dream with a deadline. If you just "wish" to accomplish some vague dream, you would find yourself wandering and so will be your time.

Write them down and review your plans

Writing each and every step of your plan towards your goals helps a lot. You can fix the deadline for each step and strive well towards getting each milestone accomplished. Then you got to review the plan at suitable intervals of time and check if it is going right or you need some amendment.

Checklist for every task

Before you start any new task as per your plans, make a checklist of the sub-tasks you would review later if they were accomplished or not. This ensures that you did not miss anything. Also, write down the deadline along the side of each of the sub-task to be accomplished and keep on ticking every time you get that mini-task executed. This makes sure that you develop a momentum in your work. By and by your productivity and velocity of doing things would get dramatically increased.

The amazing powers of cushion-time

The concept of "cushion time" is a part of planning for any project and it is the extra time that must be budgeted to take care of the unforeseen contingencies that can happen.

Average people are ruined by the unexpected events, but smart people (secretly) remain prepared for them by keeping the cushion time in their schedule. They expect the best and remain prepared for the worst. Even if the worst or unexpected things don't happen, the cushions always give them some more time to take it to perfection or simply for relaxing and relieving the work stress, which ultimately also leads to overall perfection.

Have you observed that when you plan to get to your office by 9 am, you mostly get there by around 9:15 am? Or have you felt bad when you had planned to finish a task by Tuesday and actually finish it by Wednesday or Thursday?

According to the cushion principle, if one wants to effectively plan for a future task or event, one should (secretly) aim to (genuinely) finish that task within any time before the deadline which has been stated publicly.

So next time, you should secretly aim to genuinely reach to your office by 8:45 am. 2 things can happen this way: either some unexpected event occurs (like a traffic jam) and it wastes your 15 minutes, you still reach your office by 9 am, or nothing unexpected occurs and you can move at your own pace and not at all be rushed about running late and feel relaxed and more productive throughout your day.

How successful people make use of cushion time?

1. Aiming secretly and finishing genuinely

This is the principle that great leaders and managers follow. If they are organising a meeting that is going to publicly last 1 hour, they would secretly aim to genuinely finish it within 45 or 50 minutes. This way they would maintain the principle that "brevity is the soul of wit" as well as ensure that their next event is going to start exactly on time. The top students also follow this cushion principle and aim to prepare for their exam as if it is in the next month while actually it would be held after 3 months. This way they gain an edge over other (even more intelligent) students, who are still striving to complete their syllabus even few minutes before the exam.

2. Lengthening the total duration by adding cushions

An activity/project/goal is composed of many individual tasks to be completed. Sometimes, the successful people are not sure that whether a task can be completed in the allocated time or not. What they do is they add an extra cushion and thereby, lengthen the total duration. No doubt, the extra task duration delays the completion date of that particular task and thus, there may be delay in the project finish date, but this way they feel more certain that the task in question can be completed in the estimated time. This thing has a clear advantage over not getting things done at all or delaying it to months and even years.

3. Using the Slack Time

When the successful people schedule their tasks, they usually find that some tasks depend on other tasks to finish and thus can't start for now. This automatically results in time cushions between tasks. This is called as the slack time.

What poor achievers do in slack time is that they become stressed on why the last task isn't finishing quickly and eagerly keep waiting for it to finish with frowned eyebrows.

What average achievers do in slack time is that they just sit back and relax and refresh themselves during this slack time. This is of course better than getting stressed.

However, how high achievers make better use of this slack time is by collecting the resources, charting out new and better alternatives for the further tasks and even doing some doable future tasks while being relaxed and in no hurry.

4. The task contingencies

When the successful people have risky tasks in their

project, they assign specific time cushions to them called as task contingencies. It differs from using the cushions to increase the overall duration of a task as mentioned above, because the contingency amounts remain separate from the tasks. If they completely have no idea that how long a particular task might take to get completed, they can assign a time cushion as a contingency to make sure that they can complete the task by the projected finish date. If they later get new information that lets them estimate the duration of this particular task accurately, they reduce or remove this contingency. Thus, time contingency being a separate amount, is a more flexible approach than increasing task duration and should be used in tasks we have no idea about how long they would take. Less risky tasks should be managed by simply increasing the task duration by introducing cushions.

5. Time cushions as buffers

Now, sometimes the high achievers are uncertain about how long an activity will take overall. They manage it by inserting time cushions as buffers between the individual tasks of the activity. The good thing about the buffers is that they remain as the explicit time cushions, separate from individual tasks and when the task following the buffer starts, they disappear. While the start time/date of the next task reflects the actual start, the buffer assigned before that time/date becomes meaningless. They may sometimes use some of the allocated buffer time to start their next task earlier than originally scheduled. This way they may be able to reassign additional buffer time later in the project in case the risks have increased.

Plan, sleep, wake up and execute

The best time to make a to-do list for the day is before going to bed on the previous day. This practice is common among the successful people. Although a small group of successful people wake up early and make their to-do list then only, however the former process is considered better. This is because of the two reasons: You can get a refreshing sleep as you know what you have to do and how to do it on the next day. You won't find yourself being restless due to the thoughts of what would you do on the next day. The second thing you can ensure this way is that you just have to wake up tomorrow and start right away on doing what you have planned. You don't waste time on making plans early in the morning and utilize whole of your fresh brain energy in actually executing the task.

The question to be asked to yourself

There are two questions you need to ask yourself for ensuring maximum productivity of your efforts. These are the questions (or different versions of these same questions) which every successful individual asks his/her mind:

1. When you are not clear what needs to be done now: What is the best use of my time right now?

2. When a new task shows up while you are involved in your usual planned task: Is this the best use of my time right now?

Don't delay it, Delegate it

Sometimes you may feel that some task of yours cannot be completed right on time due to your over busy schedule. You might think of delaying them and eventually at the end of the week you get scared with the huge pile of tasks that you delayed. The best possible way is to delegate these tasks to the people who can do them as good as you can or even better than you can.

Richard Branson knew, from the very age of 16, the importance of delegation. By the age of 23 when he had a large and complex business, he had already learnt how to delegate. He still relies on a terrific team to help him run all of Virgin's operations. He is surely referred to as the master of delegation.

Where to and where not to multitask

Although considered as a method of improving brain power in the recent past, new studies have showed that our brains aren't designed at all for multitasking. In fact when we feel like we are multitasking, our brains are just shifting from one task to another. This reduces our efficiency of getting the individual tasks done as well as reduces your IQ by 10 points by the end of the day of multitasking.

However, there are moments during the day where it would be stupid to just be involved in one such task which doesn't require much concentration, like time spent in the plane for travel, time spend in waiting outside your dentist's or some official's room, and so on. Wouldn't it be better to read some good book or even concentrate your mind on formulating plans for some new goal during this time? This seems similar to the slack time we discussed before. So, the bottom-line here is that the tasks which require high concentration should be dealt with separately and with complete focus on each task. The ones which require just waiting and sitting back have room for accumulating some other task in their respective time.

Where to and where not to procrastinate

Frankly speaking, you should never ever procrastinate if you want to achieve something great. However, in certain situations, when you are caught between the deadline and the shallow sea of time, there you are bound to procrastinate or delay some of the tasks. In this situation, the high achievers procrastinate the low value tasks but the low achievers procrastinate the high value tasks and thus, follow the path of least resistance.

Chunk it down

Henry Ford said, "The biggest goal can be achieved if you simply break it down into enough small parts." So, if you just focus on the next step towards your goal, you would see how this next step would magically take care of your next-nextstep. Most of the people keep thinking on "how" to achieve their goal, which is located at the top of the staircase, and feel discouraged every time they think about the huge burden of so many steps they have to climb. The successful people only focus on one step at a time with complete faith and focussing on only "what" is that they want to achieve.

Blocks of time

You might have observed that if you think you would take three hours to read one chapter of a book - that is how much it takes. If you think that it would take you just one hour to do the same task, one hour is the time it would take you to complete it. So, keeping this thing in mind, successful people create blocks each of 30 minutes or 1 hour and complete their sub tasks within that particular time limit. So, you can have 3- 4 blocks of time before leaving for office, one more in office if you arrive early, other one during the lunch break and next one if you stay for sometime at the office after the usual office hours. Then, if you take a nap after your usual office hours, you can have still 3-4 blocks of time in case you are highly enthusiastic towards accomplishing any goal.

Ingvar Kamprad, who started IKEA as a mail-order business from the small village of Agunnaryd in 1943 used to wake up at 6AM every day. He believed and practised that we should divide our lives into blocks or units of 10 minutes and sacrifice as few of them as possible on useless and meaningless activities. Well 10 minute blocks would be difficult to handle for everyone, but 20 minute blocks or simply 1 hour blocks are comparatively more manageable in today's world.

Energy management

Dr. Mehmet Oz is a surgeon who performs 250 open-heart surgeries in a year. He hosts his own popular TV show. He is also a professor and chairman of surgery department in a hospital. He is also a prolific writer and a balanced family man with four children.

His manages his tasks in a similar way as Ingvar Kamprad does. Nevertheless, he focuses on energy management rather than on time management.

He tries to devote his time to tasks that inspire and energize him. Everybody has natural crests and troughs of energy that dictate when they work best. For some, early mornings are sacred, for others the late hours of the night are when they're most productive. Dr. Oz manages his tasks well taking these moments of high energy, maximizes them and cuts out tasks that don't boost his energy and rather drag down his energy.

Balance

Successful people aren't overly busy or they don't work at a stretch for 24 hours daily, and their personal lives aren't spoiled as is the common notion. Instead, they know what it means to have a balance in their lives. They keep track of their time and manage to spend sufficient time in their work and their personal and social realms.

Be organized

Having an organized work place, an organized pattern of work and organized thoughts, ideas, beliefs and plans accompanied with organized action is the hallmark of successful people.

Avoiding interruptions

Your frequent telephone calls, emailing, texting and unexpected visits and meetings can make you less productive during the day. Successful people always bunch these tasks up for a particular time of the day especially when their high priority tasks are over.

Bunch those bananas up

The most productive people not only bunch the "not so important" tasks together, but they also batch their high priority tasks together. This becomes the reason for their high productivity as their mind doesn't have to shift from one type of task to another.

Waking up early in the morning

Most of the successful people wake up early in the morning at around 4:30 to 5:30 am and start working on their tasks right from that time. During morning, the brain's efficiency is the highest and of course it is fresh after a long night sleep. **Indra Nooyi**, the CEO of PepsiCo, wakes up at 4 a.m. and is in the office at exactly 7 a.m. Disney CEO **Bob Iger** wakes up at 4:30 am to read, and Square CEO **Jack Dorsey** gets up from bed at 5:30 to jog and maintain his health while others poor achievers keep snoring.

Chapter Thirty-Two
FOLLOWING ONE'S BLISS

Follow your bliss and the Universe will open doors where there were only walls - Joseph Campbell

Joseph John Campbell was an American writer, mythologist and lecturer. He is best known for his work in comparative religion and comparative mythology. His work being vast covers many aspects of the human experience and the historians have often summarized his philosophy by his phrase: "Follow your bliss."

Almost everyone always says, "Follow your dreams!" but does anyone do it? The reason why most of the people don't do it is because they don't believe that their dreams can ever turn into reality. Life often interjects, bills frequently pile up, and sometimes you would have to do jobs that you don't want to do but you just want to somehow make it through the day. The people who you find successful after following their dreams were just normal people like others yesterday. The only difference they made is that they believed they could follow their dreams while you may have not done so.

There are a number of reasons to break the usual trend, to

follow your dreams, and to live the life you have always wanted:

1. Living your dream makes your life worth living.

It is your dream that keeps you going even in the worst days when you are struggling. It makes you rise early in the morning and persist, persevere and work hard until you achieve it. You would rejoice the whole journey of reaching your goal and your happiness would be multiplied when you would actually reach your goal and start living the dream.

Walt Disney was a boy brought up in a farm. He used to draw pictures for his neighbors for money. Then, he used to be a cartoonist for the school newspaper. He just loved drawing cartoons. Disney even went through the worst phase of his life when he was jobless and no one was hiring him. He still didn't quit following his bliss. He was helped by his brother with his job search. Finally, he went from rags to riches by starting out with the advertisements and then going on to animate his own cartoons.

2. You can be a source of inspiration to others.

You would give others that hope and the sense of belief in one's dreams when you succeed in following them. The successful people out there today share their success stories with everyone because they know that what following one's dream means for a person and they want all of the humanity to listen to their hearts and follow where the dreams want to take them. Then only this earth can be a better place to live in.

Henry Ford was yet another farm boy who followed his bliss and revolutionized the transportation industry in America. He was deeply interested in mechanics from a young age. When he was only 15, he dismantled and then reassembled a small pocket watch his father had given him. He went out being an apprentice machinist and personally started experimenting on gasoline engines. These engines were the beginning of his vast Ford Empire. As per Forbes in 2008, his net worth is a cool $188.1 billion. His dream of belting the entire earth got manifested as you can see Ford cars on almost every road.

3. You'll meet other dream seekers.

You will attract other people with the same values and interests. They will keep the sense of motivation in you alive. It was Paul Allen, the school friend of **Bill Gates**, who shared a common dream with him and they met even after they had parted their ways and succeeded in achieving what the world is today praising them about.

4. When you work on something you don't like, your whole life would be hell.

You would find yourself counting the minutes sometimes, your efficiency would be low, you can suffer from various kinds of mental ailments and you would fear waking up in the morning.

5. The internal happiness that comes along with the process of following one's dreams is the eternal one.

Even if you literally "die" following your dreams, there will be a smile on your lips in the coffin because you had already imagined what you wanted to have and were in the pursuit of your dreams. That is far better than dying while having "grudges" with and "hatred" about yourself for not following your dreams and about the world for not letting you follow your dreams.

Steve Jobs frequently used to say, "Love what you do." He believed that if we don't love doing what we are doing or do what we love to, we are going to quit or burn out if we choose to stay. Even when Jobs was feeble and weak due to cancer, he still used to assemble his strength to go to board meetings and even on the launches of any new Apple product.

Oprah Winfrey believes that we know we are on the road to success if we would do our job and not be paid for it. She feels that when we are doing what we are meant to do, everyday feels like a bonus regardless of what we are getting paid. When we do what we love to do, the rest of the things like money, fame and honour come along with it naturally because this way we are already at our highest potentials.

6. The best thing about dreams is that they are like fingerprints.

Every individual has, in one way or the other way, his or her own distinct dreams. If you are not going to follow your own dreams, who is going to follow them for you? Your dreams would become bubbles in the air that will soon burst after you die or lose motivation.

7. You can prove all those people wrong that stopped you from following your dream.

They either did it because they didn't know how to follow their own dreams or how to follow this dream of yours, or they simply don't want you to succeed in your attempts of being great.

. . .

8. Following your bliss will make yourself and your family proud.

You can pursue more goals when you achieve one and even help people achieve theirs. You will enjoy this kick and rejoice every time you remember the kick that comes when your goals are achieved.

9. Surely the life is short and you live only once.

It is too short to first do what the society acclaims as achievable and then do something which you love. Start right away working on what you dream of and this is the principle which every successful individual knows. **JK Rowling** finished writing her first story when she was just six years old. You have hardly found any individual who followed his/her dreams, achieved immense wealth, fame, and honour and then suddenly gave everything away because he/she thought that he/she was wrong to follow the dreams. Although it is true that people realise their ultimate dream sooner or later but they only achieve that ultimate dream when they have mastered how to achieve the dream that was perceived before.

Chapter Thirty-Three
GRATITUDE AND GIVING

Cultivate the habit of being grateful for every good thing that comes to you, and to give thanks continuously. And because all things have contributed to your advancement, you should include all things in your gratitude. - Ralph Waldo Emerson

Successful people approach their life with a sense of gratitude. They are constantly aware of the wonderful things in their life. Since they enjoy the fruits of their successes and have a feeling of thankfulness about them all the time, they seek out more success. And as someone has said, "whatever you think and thank about, you bring about", they attract more and more successes. They never get disappointed by failure and consider it as a stepping stone as their hearts are filled with the happiness of gratitude.

Filling a bucket with a hole at bottom

However, the people who lack gratitude are never happy in a true sense. In case they somehow manage to succeed at one task of their goal, they don't enjoy it. They believe that they would be happy only when they get a string of successes.

It is similar to filling a bucket with a huge hole at the bottom with water. These types of people get discouraged by even the smallest failure.

The heavenly feeling of gratitude

The feeling of gratitude has its meaning beyond the boundaries of formal appreciation for kindness. We cannot fruitfully bring more assets into our lives unless we have a feeling of thankfulness for the assets we already possess. It never matters how small those assets are. It starts from a "feeling" of satisfaction that a "sense" of inner joy comes into being. While this "feeling" is a creator of more wealth and successes, this "sense" gives birth to more happiness on the outside. The reason, as to why some established entrepreneurs fall into bankruptcy, is that they lack gratitude. They constantly start to feel ungrateful for what they have, feel that they are having earned very less (in spite of riches), until they get buried into graveyards of poverty with the soul-contaminating soil of thanklessness over them. So, we should start our day with this feeling of gratitude and see how we attract miracles throughout the day.

The power of giving

Successful people also know the power of "giving" along with the gratitude. They give away thousands of dollars in charity and start earning millions and give away millions and then earn billions. Whenever **Bill Gates** donates any amount of money, he feels like he just saved someone's life and he really enjoys this feeling. Successful people also give their services to help people, share their knowledge and success secrets and the only thing they never give is "giving up!" **Steve Jobs** believed that it did not matter to him if he was the richest man in the cemetery. However, it mattered to him if he went to the bed at night and say to himself that he had done something wonderful with a sense of gratitude.

The more we celebrate, the more there is to celebrate

Oprah Winfrey also believes in the amazing powers of gratitude. She feels that the more we praise and celebrate our life, the more there is in the life to celebrate. According to her, if we remain thankful for what we have now, we will be ending up having more and more of it. In case our concentration jumps onto pondering, on a constant basis, what we don't have, we will never ever have enough of what we desired.

Serving others is the secret

As per **Henry Ford**, the secret to success lies in serving others. When a business is devoted to service, we would have embarrassingly large profits. Wealth is like happiness, it is never attained when sought after directly. In fact, wealth comes as a by-product of providing a useful service.

Trading expectation for appreciation

The world famous motivational speaker, **Tony Robbins** says that we should use the power of gratitude and appreciation for magnetizing more and more of what we want into our lives. He teaches it to be done in a unique way. He wants us to trade our expectation for appreciation and claims that our world would changes instantly. Let us see what he means.

Of course the expectation and appreciation are two different energies that vibrate at different levels. Hence, they create different realities energetically. Expectation is a strong belief hoping something to happen or be the case in the future. When we are in the energy of expectation, whatever it is that we want, we are pushing it out into the future. Appreciation, on the other hand, refers to recognizing and enjoying the good qualities of something or someone NOW. When we appreciate something, we have a full understanding of the situation. So, with this energy of appreciation, we are in the present time. Hence, when we appreciate something as our valuable entity, even if in the present moment it is not ours, we magnetize it towards us.

Chapter Thirty-Four

WATCHFUL OVER WHICH HABITS ARE BEING FORMED

Watch your thoughts, they become words; watch your words, they become actions; watch your actions, they become habits; watch your habits, they become character; watch your character, for it becomes your destiny - Frank Jackson

One of the greatest traits of successful people is being watchful over the habits that they form. Habit is something you do daily due to the fact that you have done it over and over again in the past.

Leave the actions that can become obstacles

While successful people know the fact that any habit can be formed easily, and that habits are very hard to change, they introspect and examine their daily actions and thoughts on a constant basis. If they find that they are getting involved in something bad act (bad in the sense that it can become an obstacle in their pathway towards the goal), they leave that action at once or stop thinking that thought over and over again.

. . .

Acquiring the habits that take you towards the dreams

However, they have maintained their daily lives in such a manner that they have a constant interaction with smarter people and sometimes those people who are more successful than they are. This subconsciously affects the way they take actions and the way they think. If it seems to be going better, they continue doing the same actions and developing same beliefs which would become their habit very soon. So, they even control their habit formation process. Habits are what become the character, and by and by the destiny of the person starts getting a backward or forward shift depending upon how bad or good the habits are.

The qualities that you admire the most

Warren Buffett has a very good approach towards the process of habit formation: "Pick out a person you admire the most, and then write down why admire them. You're not to name yourself in this. And then put down the person that, frankly, you can stand the least, and write down the qualities that turn you off in that person. The qualities of the one you admire are traits that you, with a little practice, can make your own, and that, if practiced, will become habit-forming."

Chains which are too heavy to be broken

He also claims that the chains of habit are too light to be felt until they are too heavy to be broken. He keeps advising the youth that he is almost stuck to change any of his habits due to his old age now. But young people will have the habits 20 years from now that they decide to put into practice today.

. . .

Qualities mentioned in this book

If you keep on inoculating the qualities and habits of successful people mentioned in this book, these can become your habits as well. When you inoculate just one habit at a time, you would notice a change in yourself. Change is a process, not an event, so you need to be patient while developing a habit. It develops by having a positive approach towards acquiring that habit and then practising it on a constant basis for two weeks or a month (depending on how enthusiastic you are).

Chapter Thirty-Five
BEING IN CHARGE OF ONE'S OWN LIFE

If you could kick the person in the pants responsible for most of your trouble, you wouldn't sit for a month - Theodore Roosevelt.

Many of you might be living your life with a misunderstanding in mind that you are entitled to a great life. Well that is not the actual part of the misunderstanding, but you might be having a belief that somewhere there is someone or some perfect situation responsible for filling your lives with eternal happiness, opportunities, make you rich, make you famous and let you live the life you always imagine and feel excited about. Well to be truthful enough, all successful people of today and yesterday, understand/understood one important fact of life – The only person who is in-charge and responsible for your life is YOU and only YOU, and the perfect situation for taking action towards achieving your goals is NOW and only NOW!

Everyone knows it, No one applies it

Everyone knows about this fact, but only some people really apply this fact to their life and become rich (not just in monetary sense), famous and successful. **Theodore Roosevelt** was an author, naturalist, explorer, soldier, and historian who served as the 26th President of the United States of America. As mentioned above, he believed that if we could kick the person in the pants responsible for most of our trouble, we wouldn't sit for a month. You are responsible for your success as much you are responsible for your failures and troubles in life.

Rejecting the path of least resistance

Why is it, that everyone knows about this reality, still not everyone is indeed successful? Their heart knows this fact, but still tends to choose the path of least resistance. It tricks the mind of the person into thinking that external factors are the source of his/her failure, unhappiness and disappointment. However, the truth that it rejects every time is that everyone has a complete control over the quality of his/her life and that the external factors don't determine how you live.

Being responsible for one's own failure

Only that person who takes full responsibility for the thoughts he/she thinks, the images he/she visualizes, and the actions he/she takes becomes successful. He/she doesn't waste his/her energy and time in complaining and blaming the external factors for any setback in his/her life. If fact, he/she holds himself/herself responsible for that failure, evaluates those experiences that held him/her back and decides, with firm determination what he/she needs to change for driving successfully over those speed-breakers the next time. He/she jumps out of his/her comfort zone and takes risks in order to create the life he/she wants to live and fulfil the dreams, not caring how meagre or how large those dreams may be.

The blame game
Sometimes you just start blaming your parents for letting you choose only their prescribed way of living the life. However, this is partly true. Some parents, mostly in developing countries, do force their children not to take untrodden pathways, but there are a huge number of people from the developing nations who choose to follow their dreams by being in-charge of their own lives and create history.

Stop blaming and start steering
Anne Frank was a teen girl who transformed the pain of her secret world into such a memoir that touched and is still touching a million hearts. She believed that parents can only give good advice or put their children on the right paths, but the final forming of a person's character lies in their own hands. Furthermore, **JK Rowling** claims that she doesn't blame her parents for anything bad that happened in her life. She believes that there is an expiry date for blaming your parents for steering you in the wrong direction. She discovered that she had a strong will and more discipline than she had ever suspected. The moment you are old enough to take the wheel, responsibility lies with you. If you are still blaming someone else for not letting you find your own dream, and bringing the dream into your life, you need to grab the wheel as you are old enough to drive. So, stop blaming and you can start the steering of your life.

. . .

You – the master of your fate, the captain of your soul

You have to be in charge of your own life. You are the master of your fate. You are the captain of your soul. If you believe that God has written everything in the form of lines of luck in your palm, and you don't need to do anything or take any action or think about your dream anymore, then ask yourself, why has He blessed you with the two hands, the two legs, the mind to take decisions, the heart to enclose and get close to dreams? What happened to free will that you are guaranteed from your God? Aren't you shaping your destiny in the moments of making a decision? The fact is that people seldom understand the amazing phenomenon of luck properly. "Luck" has become a target of blaming for the low achievers when they fail, while "Free-will", "Choice", "Decision" have become the most powerful weapons of high achievers.

Control your attitude and master the change

Sometimes your health runs down or the plans go wrong or the people you trusted deceived you. Still YOU and only YOU are the one who can get up and fix everything bad in your life. No one is going to do it for you. **Brain Tracy** believes that may be sometimes you cannot control what happens to you, but what you can control is your attitude toward what is happening to you. When you do that, you will be mastering the change rather than allowing it to master you.

Use the pain and pleasure instead of having them use you

Tony Robbins knows that one of the secrets of success is learning how to use the pain and pleasure instead of having pain and pleasure use you. Even Albert Einstein, the wisest man and genius of the 20th century, believed in having personal responsibility. Einstein understood that man has a bad habit of attributing his problems to his environment. He advocated that man should cease doing that and learn again to exercise his will.

The person who knows how to bend the Universe

Jeff Bezos, CEO and President of Amazon.com focussed more on taking action, any action rather than sitting back, lamenting your bad luck and watching other people taking action towards their dreams. He believes that it is only through deliberate action that we can bend the universe to our will. He rejects the common misunderstanding about taking action: that we must know the exact right action to take before wearing our shoes and doing anything. This way of thinking leads to "analysis paralysis" and inaction.

Be responsible for becoming proactive and productive

When we completely understand that we are in-charge of and responsible for our own lives, we come to know about the power of being proactive. That is what Jeff Bezos did. In 1994, when Jeff Bezos faced with the biggest decision of his life that should he quit his "well-paying" job as NYC hedge fund manager or should he create an online bookstore, the thing he dreamt about but knew nothing much about how to do it? Well, he decided to go big, started with buying the domain rights to Amazon.com and thus, carved his name in gold in the book of history.

Chapter Thirty-Six
JOVIAL

Honest good humor is the oil and wine of a merry meeting, and there is no jovial companionship equal to that where the jokes are rather small and laughter abundant - Washington Irving

Successful people are not just money machines or extremely hungry wolves for fame or sociopaths who only believe in dragging money and fame towards themselves. In fact, these types of temporarily successful people soon face failure. The real successful people are jovial, and know the meaning of being cheerful and friendly towards people as they are aware of the fact that money alone doesn't matter in success. It is the social relationship and a positive impact they have on people's or customer's minds that matters in the long run.

The more jovial you are the more likeable you would be

Of course being bossy is an important part of the first impact you want to have on your employees, but if this quality of being "bossy bread" is not buttered with a bit of cheerfulness, you are going to lose people soon. Also, having over-buttered this authoritarian bread with excessive friendliness would make you lose control over the people and it would be difficult to obtain the control back. Successful people know how to balance these two natures and in fact they try to internally balance their dominating nature and love for people since people are smart and can catch your pretentious nature.

Being jovial allows for bonding

When you know how to make a person laugh or smile, that person immediately begins to feel as if you understand him/her. He/she begins to feel that you share a similar sense of humor and therefore are most likely to have other things in common as well. This nature helps in a business meeting, getting new opportunities, resources, or even in public speaking. Humor is a great weapon of successful people for cracking that formal wall of strictness and getting people to drop their guard. This way, they are able to attack the people they are talking to and take them for all they are worth. However, you should remember that a bad joke can kill the vibe, thus, you need to make sure that you actually are funny if you are going to be funny.

As portrayed in the movie "The Social Network", **Mark Zuckerberg** had a few friends in the beginning. However, later his jovial nature allowed him to make friends with Peter Thiel (LinkedIn) and Sean Parker (Napster) and other bigwigs of Silicon Valley. This, of course, helped him in gaining more and more opportunities and resources for enabling Facebook to be there where it stands today.

We know that **Oprah Winfrey** has a very tight circle of really close friends. Many of them were her friends before she became famous. She often advises that you need to surround yourself only with supportive and uplifting people, those who want your dreams to turn into reality as badly as you do. She also believes that we need to keep negative people at bay as they are not your friends. However, the world today is materialistic and we would tend to lose people from our lives this way. The smart way to handle this issue is to make millions of "companions" (for gaining experience) but only a few trustworthy and positive "friends" (for the real emotional bonding that one longs for).

Being cheerful relieves that load of stress

It is really good to be focussed and not to waste a single bit of time while you are working. However, successful people know that the importance of having friends, family, cracking jokes with them, and allocating time to relax. They know that the time wasted in relaxing and relieving the stress is not wasted at all. Stress incredibly damages our psyche and considerably decreases our productivity. Cheerfulness is contagious and it makes the person delivering the joke laugh too.

The cheerful guy is always invited

When someone creates a list of people he/she is going to invite to any event, the majority of the people on the list would be the ones he/she finds to be cheerful. They tend to be the life of the event and without them, the events and the parties tend to be mediocre. Similarly, people like to hang out with jovial people, those that can relieve their stress or simply put a smile on their face.

This thing would surely push you forward as you get a chance to meet and hang out with those people who are better than you. **Warren Buffet** always believed that we need to pick out those associates whose behavior is better than ours and this way we will drift in that direction.

The great networking tool

Having a good sense of humor is a great networking tool in the business world. If you are entertaining and cheerful, you are more likely to be introduced to others. You are more likely to meet the kind of people you want to meet.

A good sense of humor facilitates trust

Ask yourself, if you would like to trust someone who is pretty boring and overly formal or the one who is within the formal limits and has a good sense of humor as well? Without guessing much, you chose the second option. That is why, the salesperson are given the training of being friendly with the customers (even if the customer is a pain in the ass).

Andrew Carnegie got his initial start by earning the trust of and making friends with rich people. In particular, he got the help from Thomas A. Scott, the famous American businessperson and railroad executive of that time. Carnegie was invited to invest in companies by Thomas Scott. Although he had less capital for investment, Scott would also provide him the capital and a very friendly way of repaying that debt. Finally when Carnegie got involved in Iron business which later became steel, and in turn Carnegie Steel, he was quite wealthy and an independent businessman.

Being jovial increases group effectiveness and productivity

You jovial nature creates an atmosphere that is easier to work in. If you lightly poke small mistakes instead of scolding badly, the people will be less afraid of making them. They can easily think outside the box and thus increase the overall productivity. Smiling or laughing makes our brains release dopamine, which in turn literally increases the creativity and productivity.

Jovial people are more outgoing

Being jovial gives you more confidence and efficient social skills. You become confident enough to face every situation joyfully. You are more likely to interact with new people as you know that you have the ability to make people smile or laugh. One of the most important characteristics of successful people is being outgoing. If you feel you are comfortable enough to approach new people that you do not know, you can increase your networking business and pick up potential customers or clients. **Richard Branson** advocates that we should travel often and meet as many people as we can. According to him, this is how he came by some of the best ideas and suggestions for his business.

Chapter Thirty-Seven

KNOWLEDGEABLE, INNOVATIVE AND CREATIVE

Creativity is just connecting things. When you ask creative people how they did something, they feel a little guilty because they didn't really do it, they just saw something. It seemed obvious to them after a while. That's because they were able to connect experiences they've had and synthesize new things. - Steve Jobs

The golden sword of knowledge

Being educated is different than being knowledgeable. In this era, we see people, who are having so many degrees and medals from top schools/colleges/universities, are being hired by other people of no or low education background to fulfil their dreams. However, we often perceive this thing wrongly and in a manner different from actual reality. It is not the level of education that matters, it is the level of knowledge and skills one has that matters in every field. The degrees from top universities can definitely fetch you a multitude of opportunities, but to persist and get promoted in your respective field, you need a wide deal of knowledge, skills, and often tips and tricks which are never ever taught in institutions.

. . .

Those who innovate

Being innovative is also one of the attributes of the successful people. The know how fruitful it can be to think out of the box and smartly take risks and thus land up inventing their own methods, brand new products and extremely different and productive visions for the future. Only these types of people create history, and not the ones who just take degrees from top universities without getting their skills build up.

The power of creativity

Now let's talk about the power of creativity, which is a sort of inborn nature everyone of us is bestowed with. Children are highly creative and during the time they grow, they are taught that the society and parents unknowingly teach them that it is not smart to think something new, that you cannot follow the path which has no footprints and you should not think those thoughts which take you away from the usual path you are (forcibly) destined to follow. Only those who thought out of the box and went ahead, create history. The rest of the people are either born great or born to serve the great in one or the other way.

Education gives you an edge

However, there are people who have had a good academic performance and developed skills in true sense, not just for the sake of studying. **Bill Gates** scored 1590 on his Scholastic Aptitude Test (SAT) when the top score for the test then was just 1600. This helped him get enrolled at Harvard College in the year 1973. Before the mid-1990s, a SAT score of 1590 roughly corresponded to an IQ of 170. Even before that, Gates had discovered his interest in software while he was just 13 and studying at private Lakeside School. He started writing his own computer programmes since this young age and sold his first computer program for $4,200 at the young age of 17. It was a time-tabling system for his high school.

Innovate on a constant basis

Bill Gates being the co-founder of software company Microsoft, didn't stick to just selling Microsoft software. He continued being the king of computer industry by introducing and constantly updating his innovative products such as Windows and Xbox.

Think smart

Steve Jobs used his creativity so efficiently that was he is known to be one of the greatest thinkers of all time. He was a showman and knew people were doubtful to new ideas. What he would do is that he would put on a show for the purpose of uncovering and demonstrating his inventions. He used to do so in order to make common people understand his vision and simply get excited.

Never hesitate to steal great ideas

As a company, Apple didn't necessarily invent things—instead what they did is that they used the existing concepts and products and made them seem phenomenal. For instance, Steve Jobs got the concept of a visual-based operating system from Xerox, and called it 'Xerox PARC'. He took the same concept for producing the original Mac, with some really cool enhancements and his perfectly smart vision. He even revealed the fact that while those who copy are good artists;

those who steal are great artists. So, Steve Jobs never hesitated in stealing great ideas.

Think out of the box

Steve Jobs also used to think out of the box in terms of market research. While famous entrepreneurs spend millions of dollars for market research and in knowing the mass psychology, he believed that we can't just ask the customers what they want and then try to give that to them because by the time we get it built, they will want something new. In fact, he obstinately relied on his own instinct and refined the existing technologies, developed brand new products out of them and packaged them in a way that people would love to use.

Imitate but uniquely

However, sometimes it is better to know how mass psychology works but you still don't need market research for it. **Jeff Bezos** claims that it is okay to be unique but it is even better to take something that has been already proven to work and put a unique twist on it. He claims that at Amazon.com, they watch their competitors and learn from them. They do it by observing and noting down the things that they were doing for their customers and then copying those things as much as they can.

Being experienced matters

Richard Branson is the only entrepreneur to have built 8 separate billion-dollar companies in 8 different industries and he literally had no degree in business management. He acquired the knowledge of all do's and don'ts of business from his own experience, taking action and taking risks.

The Emotional Intelligence

The other important realm in this big field of knowledge, innovation and creativity is the Emotional Intelligence (EI). EI monitors feelings, boosts self-awareness, improves the much needed communication skills and increases the social awareness of a human being. It also helps in strengthening mediation skills and helps to prevent conflict. **Oprah's** leadership style is a perfect reflection of emotional intelligence. She is well aware of her own vision. This has led her to achieve her dreams. Her empathy and listening skills have enabled her to motivate others.

Henry Ford dreamed of a "horseless carriage" and went to work with what little tools he possessed. Although uneducated, he was having a great sense of curiosity and once took apart and put together his brother's toy only to know how it worked. He is known to have a high level of emotional intelligence, even before this term was coined.

Ford had an ability to understand that if you save client's' money, it made them feel more valued. He was too sensitive to the economic needs and took proper action to respond to his customers in ways that revealed his care for them. In the same way, he looked forward for maintaining the financial and work life balance needs of his employees. He even implemented positive wage and shift changes as he hoped to show understanding and appreciation toward them. Ford firmly believed that we should develop the ability to see things from the other person's point of view as well as your own.

Imagination is better than knowledge

The power of imagination has been attributed as one of the greatest powers a human mind has. Every successful person has praised the imaginative power of human mind, be it creative visualization for the life one wants or imagination of the great stories that have become the international best-selling novels or even the imagination during acquiring knowledge and developing innovative ideas or theories. **JK Rowling**, one of the most creative ladies of the modern world, believes that imagination should not be left to the children alone. She says, "We do not need magic to change the world, we carry all the power we need inside ourselves already: we have the power to imagine better". Even **Albert Einstein** said that imagination is more powerful than the knowledge.

Chapter Thirty-Eight
LEADERSHIP AND TEAM-WORK

A leader...is like a shepherd. He stays behind the flock, letting the most nimble go out ahead, whereupon the others follow, not realizing that all along they are being directed from behind - Nelson Mandela

The first step in creating a successful business venture or an organization is having a great idea, and assembling a team to turn that idea into reality. It is the ability to execute this idea that separates the entrepreneurs from the dreamers. When you step forward and make that exciting first hire, you have already taken the first step in turning yourself into a powerful leader. Every great business and every great organization started with that first step. The leadership and team-work are the essential qualities that a successful person has as he cannot do all by himself especially if he wants to achieve maximum productivity.

They have a great deal of Self Control

One of the essential leadership qualities of successful people is controlling others. However, they can't effectively control others when they can't handle their own emotions, be responsible for their actions and the words they speak out. So, all the great leaders of today or yesterday have/had established a great deal of control over their own self. This self-control gives them more might than the strength achieved in simply executing the power over others when they aren't strong enough to control their own selves.

Successful leaders have courageous hearts

Successful people need to hold the mantle of leadership and for that purpose they have held courage in their hearts: courage to face criticism boldly, courage to face failure, learn from it and move on, courage to handle great obstacles, courage to maintain a team effectively, and courage to sustain and move ahead of the competition. Whenever **Mary Kay Ash**, the famous American businesswoman and owner of Mary Kay cosmetics used to reach an obstacle, she would make her team turn that into an opportunity. **Winston Churchill**, one of the Prime ministers of UK, thought of courage as an ability to stand up, speak out, sit down and listen patiently**. W. Clement Stone** regarded the "level" of courage required to say no, to face the truth and to do the right thing, as the magic key to life, the life with integrity.

You might have probably heard about the childhood story of fearlessness of a great leader of today, **Richard Branson.** Once when Richard was young, his aunt bet him that he could never ever learn to swim when they were out for their family vacation. He failed to master the skill over and over again during the trip but tried once more every time he failed. Then, on the drive home, he asked his father to pull over the car. There was a river nearby, he straightaway jumped into it, swam, and won the bet. Branson today is a courageous business leader and believes in a philosophy of stepping out of your comfort zone and taking risks. He believes in the fact that we can't learn to walk by following the rules but we learn by doing, and by falling over.

Definiteness of Decisions, and making high quality ones

Successful leaders understand that the decision making process rests solely on their shoulders and they and the team have to live with the consequences of those decisions. They understand that their team cannot make the decision for them. It can only render advice.

Henry Ford was so firm and definite in making decisions that he was even considered obstinate at times. However, it was this firmness of his decision making process that we see the Ford cars running successfully all over the world today. Great leaders are also quick in making the calculations and arriving at a conclusion. They have habituated the process of making high quality decisions within no time by quickly going through all the information required, discussing the pros and cons with the team, mixing a bit of gut feeling and experience and standing firm on the conclusion they arrive at.

Detail oriented and effective communication

Successful leaders are very detail oriented in each task which they or their team needs to perform. They even develop a concept about various scenarios in which different problems can arise and develop specific strategies to combat such problematic scenarios if they ever happen in the future. They give detailed description of each sub-task for every person in the team. The effective communication skills enable them to interact well with the team members, collect more followers and gain more customers or clients.

. . .

Better sense of Judgment

Sometimes the successful leaders find themselves in a situation or a dilemma. Instead of getting frustrated and stressed up, they trust their instinct and the sense of judgment. They have the ability to discern right and wrong. They are really good at handling and settling the staff conflict and customer complaints.

Understanding and empathy

A good sense of understanding is yet another essential quality of successful leaders. They know that working blindly without understanding the needs of their customers or the people whom they provide the service is going to take them nowhere. They know that they need understanding to decode the signals sent across to them by their followers. Empathy is the strong force that moves every leader and his team forward along their mission or goal. The leaders who possess empathy by understanding both the logical and the emotional rationale for taking each and every decision are the ones who move forward or even take a giant leap forward successfully.

Skilful Planning

Successful leaders plan tactically and are the plan executors. Before taking any decision or making any move they plan perfectly and strategize critically with their team.

Responsibility and accountability

The courage to behold responsibility and accountability is the utmost reason why most successful people occupy leadership positions. As a leader, you are responsible and accountable for the entire actions of your team. The successful people make it clear in their minds that if things go right, their entire team will share the appreciation and honor with them but when things go wrong, the leader alone would be held responsible. Extraordinary leaders take responsibility for the performance of everyone in the team including their own.

A trusted leader, not just a leader

Successful people understand the importance of being a trusted leader. They know that this way they will get more from the people and will have a stronger following. Although it takes a long time to earn trust as it builds over time not just by saying "trust me". The flipside of the trust is that you can lose it quickly if you do something which breaks your team members' trust in you.

Good personality, positive attitude & being powerfully passionate

Good personality entails having charisma, integrity, good character, good appearance (being handsome or beautiful is not important) and self-confidence. No person, be it employee, investor or a customer would be willing to follow a timid leader who lacks good overall personality. **Warren Buffet** believes that it takes 20 years to build a reputation and only 5 minutes to ruin it. If we will think about that, we will always do things differently.

Now, you can't have a good personality and be negative about everything. Positivity in one's thoughts, words and actions enhances the personality and makes it more inspiring and charming. The other factor to be included is being powerfully passionate about your work, goals and vision. This keeps your team members motivated and renders them more productive. You start becoming a source of inspiration for them.

Team work

Successful people have the ability to hire the people that are either as smart as they are or smarter than them. Then they know how to delegate and distribute the work among the team members. While you can keep yourself busy with planning things for the next month, you would have the things for this month getting completed in a more productive way. This is the best thing about delegation.

Humility

Leadership includes building a team comprising of people who may be are smarter than you are. So if you must lead (or simply get work done) from such individuals of high intellect, then you need to be humble. You need to be humble to admit your mistakes while being a leader; you need to be humble to learn new things and to direct smarter individuals. That is why humility is regarded as one of the most important leadership traits of the people like Bill Gates, Warren Buffett, Andrew Carnegie and Mike Adenuga (the second wealthiest Nigerian).

Sense of Humor

Successful leaders are more outrageous on account of their cheerful nature, and good social skills. They always instil a positive energy in their team. They encourage their team to laugh at the mistakes instead of crying and maintain a healthy and happy environment with their good sense of humor. They even attract more people into their organization or to invest into their project by just bringing a warm smile on their face.

Commitment

Successful leaders are focussed and committed to their work. The delegate, but work themselves too with passion and commitment. They keep track of every step forward which the team makes and concentrate deeply on improving the areas in which the team fails.

Creativity and Intuition

Leadership doesn't strictly mean being strict. It should be a balanced one. Good leaders are creative themselves and the best leaders hire creative individuals who can think out of the box for them. They believe in following their natural intuition or that gut feeling which arises when every decision seems absurd and every plan feels like it is not going to work.

A deep search for talent

As already discussed above, great leaders delegate work to other smarter minds. **Steve Jobs** had unique ways to hunt for talent. He would accept invitations to lecture at universities so that he could find out his potential employees out there. Jobs is famous for personally having interviewed over 5,000 applicants during his entire lifetime. **Warren Buffet** used to look for three key attributes when hiring people integrity, intelligence and energy. He believed that if you don't see the integrity in them, the other two will kill you.

John D Rockefeller used to make sure that only the best talent was hired and also put to its highest potential in its respective field. He often gave his employees' the equity and stock ownership which acted as a huge incentive for them to work even harder as it was now a bit of their company also.

Empowering others

According to **Bill Gates**, in the coming future, the successful leaders will be those who empower others. The great leaders of today understand that you can't go forward without helping others go forward. Help your team members in their mission to go forward and instead it would lead to the increased productivity of entire team. Start empowering others and you will be empowering yourself.

Chapter Thirty-Nine
POWER OF MOTIVATING OTHERS

Motivation is the art of getting people to do what you want them to do because they want to do it - Dwight Eisenhower

There are two types of motivational powers that successful people possess. The first type is that of motivating the people to buy their products. Inciting inspiration or a surge of motivation in low achievers to make them high achievers is the other type of motivational power that they possess. While the first one is an active process, the second type is just a by product of the success they achieve and thus, usually a passive one.

The Reality Distortion Field

Steve Jobs used to create what is today known as the Reality Distortion Field (RDF). It is a phenomenon in which one's intellectual abilities and persuasion skills make other people "believe in the possibility of achieving very difficult tasks" or "do something eagerly without focussing on what and why they are doing so".

. . .

The first part of this definition

The first part of this definition was used by Jobs to bent reality in such a way that a difficult or impossible task was made to appear easy and possible. His main objective was to inspire employees and motivate them to tackle any challenging situation in pursuit of an objective or goal.

The second part of this definition

The other part of this definition was used by Jobs to sell his products. He knew how to work a crowd. He used to build excitement around technologies which, sometimes, were neither new nor world changing. When he launched the iPad 2, he focussed the attention of people to the device's "smart cover"- a square of vinyl with magnetic hinges. It even garnered significant media coverage. Even seasoned journalists of that time were not immune, who took several hours recovery time to fully make sense of what they were announcing to the general public.

Motivate them and get momentum

This power of motivating others is really very important if you have an idea that can change your life or that can bring about a significant change in the world. If you are not able to motivate people, your idea will become an air bubble and burst away. Successful authors of today usually used to have a hard time explaining the publishers how good their book is or how creative their writings are. However, once they succeeded, usually after various failed attempts, then there was no looking back. Similarly, successful businessmen have had a hard time motivating the investors about how productive their business can be. Various businessmen with best business plans and ideas fail to carry it on due to their lack of this power of motivating the investors or even the general public for selling their products. This is a quality worth having.

Chapter Forty
NEGATING THE FEAR

Inaction breeds doubt and fear. Action breeds confidence and courage. If you want to conquer fear, do not sit home and think about it. Go out and get busy - Dale Carnegie

While the fear has been called again and again as the "false experience appearing real", it is this fear that people don't touch their highest potentials. People in general fail to follow their dreams because they fear that they may fail and fear that they might lose that narrow comfort zone they are enjoying for now. Successful people negate the fear. In fact they also feel some fear and a bit nervous, but they do it anyway.

The power lies within your beliefs

Sometimes it seems that fear has such a great power that it keeps people from doing things and makes them step back when just one step could have changed their destiny. **Oprah Winfrey** tells us about the thing that has the real power. She believes that the thing we fear most has no power. In fact it is "your fear of it" that has the power. If we start facing this truth, we will set ourselves free from the captivating cage of fear. She claims, "I have a lot of things to prove to myself. One is that I can live my life fearlessly."

Handling your failure

One of the differences between high achievers and low achievers is how they handle their failure. When they have already negated the fear, their ability to effectively cope with losing, failing, and not getting what they want makes them turn the tables for them. Being able to negate all those false experiences or imagery that comes to their mind about the failure, obstacle and rejection, is an important quality for anyone to cultivate in order to achieve success and well-being. For leaders, this quality is essential. They can't delegate people for negating the fear for them. It is something located in their mind and they have to deal with it themselves boldly.

The two powerful ways – follow the first, modify the second

Failures and setbacks in life work powerfully in either one of two ways for successful people, who are always ready to face them. These can be their greatest teachers and motivators for future success. These can also keep them from ever taking a risk (and thus achieving something great) again. However, they make use of the first way in which the setbacks help and modify the second way in the sense that next time they think of taking a risk again, they do it but more smartly and with more precautions. They understand that fear is just a pseudo-glass sheet in front of them and beyond it lays the success. They break this glass of fear, climb that stepping stone to success (their previous failure) and move forward to achieve their motto in life.

Chapter Forty-One
OPTIMISM

Write it on your heart that every day is the best day in the year - Ralph Waldo Emerson

All successful people are optimistic and all optimistic people are, in one or the other way, sooner or later, successful in accomplishing their goals of life. The optimistic people tend to see the glass half full, not half empty. They believe that the whole universe is friendly towards them and helping them in achieving their dreams. However, what most of the people tend to do is they remain optimistic till whole of the journey towards their goal, and when they are about to reach the goal, they lose patience, become victims of criticism and turn their backs towards the goal when even the goal tries to pull them back but all in vain. This is the reason we don't have a success story for every dreamer and rags to riches story for everyone who is poor.

A dollar bill on the ground

When **Bill gates** was asked if he would find a dollar bill on the ground, would he bother picking it up. To this he replied that he would be more than willing to. **Warren Buffett** responded to it saying that if Bill Gates would miss he wouldn't. It is not like they are hungry for money, but it is the optimistic built up of their mind by which they perceive things that lead them to be the richest persons today.

Wisdom of early 20th century

The successful people of the early 20th century had so much optimism filled in them that many of the entrepreneurs of today regard them as their teachers even if they might not have met them directly. **W. Clement Stone** is described as a paranoid, not the one you see in asylum but an inverse paranoid. While a paranoid may believe that the world was plotting to do him harm, he believed the world was plotting to do him good. He used to look for opportunities in every challenging or difficult situation, and use those opportunities to empower and enrich him or advance his causes. **Napoleon Hill** mentioned in one of his famous books, these golden words: "Every adversity, **every failure**, and every heart-ache carries with it the **seed** of an equal or greater benefit". Similarly, **John D Rockefeller** always tried to turn every disaster into an opportunity.

Attitude to climb matters, altitude of mountain doesn't

It is really up to us that how we perceive any situation or any opportunity. **Henry Ford** was highly optimistic entrepreneur and he believed that if we think we can do a thing or we think we can't do a thing, either way, we're right. So, it is not the problem or the obstacle in our way that matters, it is our attitude towards the obstacle that matters and determines whether or not we can proceed towards our goals.

. . .

Why are we right the either way according to Ford?

In other words, the question is does positive thinking work or it is just a pseudo-scientific fact? If you think and believe that you can't do something or can't accomplish any task within a particular time, you simply won't. Now, if you think you can, or constantly put yourself into believing that you can and (and then when the mind also responds back that "yes you can"), you are more likely to do the things necessary to make it happen. Then, finally when you have a clear picture of yourself having that task accomplished (which happens by positive thinking and positively visualizing the goal as accomplished), you surely will find the path necessary to get there and will accomplish that task even before your set deadline. Thus, positive visualization helps you in defining the target so that you can shoot your automatic target recognition enabled hard-work missile. Regardless of how curved the path is, your hard-work missile will hit the target.

Chapter Forty-Two
PATIENCE, PERSEVERANCE & PERSISTENCE

I do not think that there is any other quality so essential to success of any kind as the quality of perseverance - John D Rockefeller

Good things come to those who wait. Of course patience is always rewarded and every second of hard-work is like a seed for every fruit that would be achieved when the season of patience is over, when the harvesting season of success has arrived. Perseverance is the steady patience (or patience in a long term), being patient every time until your desired goal is achieved. While both patience and perseverance are needed for short and long term success, respectively, there is a third "P" which successful people possess. It is persistence, the vehicle in which successful people arrive towards their destiny.

Three P's of Rockefeller

Let us consider these 3 P's possessed by the wealthiest man in American history (who was once regarded as the wealthiest man in the world, until someone else popped out onto top of the list from history). **John D Rockefeller** owned the world's largest oil supply called Standard Oil. He was the first man to ever accumulate one billion US dollars. He was also the primary reason a monopoly was created and, thus paved the way for upcoming billionaires, inspiring them and showing them that it was possible to create such a wealth.

Rockefeller was born in Richford, New York. He was one of six children of his parents. His did not inherit any wealth from his father who was just a travelling salesman. However, his father was a foe of conventional morality and used to find schemes and tricks he could use in order to avoid hard work or any work at all. His mother struggled a lot in order to maintain financial stability in their home, especially when John's father was gone for weeks at a time. John went through school. He then got a simple job as a bookkeeper earning just $50 in 3 months.

As discussed before, when John was still young, he made his mind to achieve 2 goals in life: First was to make one million dollars, and second was to live up to 100 years. So, in 1859, he decided to create a business with a friend named Maurice B. Clark. The two established a firm and built an oil refinery. Slowly and gradually, Rockefeller was able to establish the Standard Oil Company. He kept moving forward with patience, perseverance and persistence and became the world's first billionaire. While he just remained 3 years short of his second goal (lived till 97 years), his first goal made his name synonymous with "billionaire" and not just "millionaire".

The vision for future

Bill Gates was highly intelligent right from his childhood. When Bill's parents came to know about their son's intelligence, they decided to enrol him in a school which was known for its intense academic environment. That was, indeed the most important decision in Bill's life as here he was first introduced to computers. Bill Gates and his friends were so much interested in computers that they formed the "Programmers Group" in late 1968. They found a new way to apply their computer skills in the University of Washington. Then in next year, they were selected as programmers in Information Sciences Inc. in which they were selected as programmers and agreed to give them royalties, whenever it made money from any of the their program.

He kept on moving forward slowly and gradually and this time formed a new company Traf-O-Data with his close friend, Allen. Together, they developed a small computer which was used to measure traffic flow and earned around $20,000 from this project. Gates left the college and the era of Traf-O-Data came to an end. In 1973, he got selected in Harvard University in 1973, but he didn't know what to do and enrolled his name for pre-laws and signed up for one of Harvard's toughest mathematics courses. Although he did well over there, he couldn't find it interesting too. He used to spend many long nights in front of the school's computer and then be asleep for the next day in class. But after leaving school, he found himself lost from the world of computers. However, there remained a link - his close friend Paul Allen. He often used to discuss new ideas for future projects with Allen and the possibility of starting a new business one fine day. Allen constantly kept on pushing Bill for opening a new software company.

Bill was able to change his mind and strive towards accomplishing their mission, so within a year, he dropped out from Harvard. He co-founded what we today know as

Microsoft with Allen. They developed a vision: "A computer on every desk and Microsoft software on every computer", accomplished it and surely the rest of the things like money, fame and honor came along with the process of accomplishing their mission. It was the lifelong persistence and perseverance that made them live by their ideas and dreams.

Willing to go the extra mile

Steve Jobs was an ardent believer in the power of persistence. He was always willing to go the extra mile and to be better than he was the day before. He was fully convinced that about half of what separates the successful entrepreneurs from the non-successful ones is pure perseverance.

We already discussed that Steve Jobs built a company that he was fired from. Yes, he was first able to bring himself from a poor guy to the one who developed an idea, bring Apple from an idea to an empire and then eventually lose it all. However, he did not lose hold of his persistence and perseverance. He had developed a mindset of success and found it around every corner. When Steve was sort of fired from his company, Apple, he teamed up with a little company Pixar, went ahead, brought himself in power again and regained back the control of Apple. The take home message here is that it is not worthy that you climb a mountain, be famous for it and are be at dispense of others who can throw you down the cliff. Instead, the successful people gain mastery over climbing the first time they climb, remain persistent and so, it is you and only you who can allow yourself to be unsuccessful. Unfair circumstances are sometimes there only in the process of making you stronger as they say what doesn't kill you, makes you stronger.

. . .

Nothing can take place of persistence

According to the President **Calvin Coolidge**, there is nothing in this world can take the place of persistence. Talent will not; nothing is more common than unsuccessful men with talent. Genius will not; unrewarded genius is almost a proverb. Education will not; the world is full of educated derelicts. Persistence and determination are omnipotent. The slogan 'press on' has solved and always will solve the problems of the human race. Persistent people keep on moving forward, even when they are faced with challenges. When they face doors slammed in their face, when their start-up faces setbacks and when failures occur when they were close to success, they still remain motivated and happily persistent keeping the "end in mind" and not the obstacles.

Drive, determination and persistence

Mark Zuckerberg's most important qualities as a successful entrepreneur include drive, determination and persistence. This is demonstrated by his early on relentless coding to launch Facebook to catch the Winklevoss brothers off guard, by adding colleges, by attacking MySpace, by defending against the lawsuit from the twins and by maintaining the reputation of Facebook as the leading social networking website.

The mindset of Buffett

Warren Buffett used to work in his grandfather's grocery shop. His millionaire mindset made him to crave for money but he could not find himself any good source of earning other than selling cold drinks, weekly magazines, stamps and chewing gums door to door. He persisted hard and even didn't mind delivering newspapers. Then finally Buffett along with one if his friends invested $25 for buying a pinball machine that they installed in a barber's shop. They started generating good income out of that machine and then installed some more machines in other barber shops. He was just 11years old when he purchased his first shares for himself and for his sister. During his graduation when he was 20, he had saved $9,800, he went to meet Graham who was on the board of GEICO insurance, but was plainly rejected. He thought about increasing his skills on investment and began to pursue classes on "Investment principles". During this time, he also purchased a gas station, which, however didn't turn out to be much profitable.

Buffett's company grew to six partnerships operating the whole year. He was introduced to Charlie in 1959 and the company was named Sanborn Map Company. Slowly and gradually he started extending and expanding his business and made himself to have a good position on the Board of Sanborn.

Buffett didn't stop here and it was in 2008 when he was declared as the richest person in the world. He even didn't stop here and went on to become a billionaire with his company valuing approximately US$62 billion. Even when he donated billions to the charity in 2009, he was still ranked as the second richest man in the United States with a net worth of US$37 billion.

The dresses made out of potato sacks

The women today are highly inspired by the achievements of **Oprah Winfrey**. Many of them aren't aware of the fact that she didn't grow in the lap of luxury and was born to a housemaid and a coal miner. She is even known to have had dresses that were made out of potato sacks and also was molested by her relatives. She strived hard and entered the world of media after getting the job of a news-reader in a local black radio station. Her perseverance gave her a golden opportunity of hosting a cooking show (of which she knew nothing about) and then got her first talk-show in Chicago. After that, there was no looking back for this great personality. Oprah once said, "You CAN have it all. You just can't have it all at once." So we must understand that the lack of instant success is not same as failure as is the common notion.

His pursuit of Happiness

Chris Gardner is the personality whose life has inspired the Will Smith-starrer super hit movie 'The Pursuit of Happyness'. Chris was physically abused by his stepfather as a child and even placed in a foster home. While raising his kid, Gardner struggled with homelessness. He survived this worst phase of his life by the strength of the lessons of persistence and pressing hard and just forward, everyday and everytime, that he had learnt from his mother. These lessons were the reason that he went from rags to riches by building himself successfully to be the CEO

Women aren't weak for having persistence

JK Rowling's mother died in 1990 and she got divorced in 1993. She even suffered from clinical depression, but still didn't give up on her dream. Her life was like hell and she and her daughter were living on welfare until she finished the first book in her famous series, "Harry Potter and the Philosopher's Stone" in 1997. She even used to write it on scraps of tissue paper from the numerous cafes they visited to let her daughter sleep. Her net worth today is over $1 billion with over 400 million books and her name in the hearts of every child, teen and even adults. The bottom line here is that women, whom some ignorant folks consider weak, can face harsh internal (clinical depression) and external (divorce, homelessness, a daughter to support) problems boldly and persist towards achieving their dream and achieve it.

Chapter Forty-Three

QUICK-WITTED

Wit beyond measure is a man's greatest treasure - J.K. Rowling

Successful people are a treasure of wisdom and they are quick-witted too. Unless they have developed an ability to think or respond quickly and effectively, they can't stand the high competition of success. They even know the importance of making quick decisions and taking action quickly.

The farsighted quick-witted Gates

Bill Gates was once being interviewed by some college students. During the interview, he was asked about his view on piracy. He replied that it didn't matter for him if Asians or Africans use pirated software, but if they do then they should use the pirated software of only WINDOWS. When asked why so, he replied that they don't pay for the software right now but when will, it'll be to Microsoft.

The Rich neighbour and the 2 thieves

Microsoft was the first and only company which was developing apps for the first Mac before it was even released. Although Xerox invented the graphical user interface, the engineers at Apple saw it on a visit to the Xerox PARC Center. Due to their interaction with the Mac team, Microsoft learnt the secret sauce of GUI and then came up with Windows. **Steve Jobs** claimed that Microsoft stole Apple's ideas for the GUI. Steve Jobs was enraged and ordered **Bill Gates** to come to California to meet him. When Gates arrived, Jobs said: "You ripped us off! We trusted you, and you ripped us!" To this, the quick-witted Bill Gates replied: "Well, there's another way of looking at it, Steve. Let us assume that both of us have this rich neighbour called Xerox and I broke in to steal the TV, only to find out that you had already taken it."

Just show up and be quick-witted

Sometimes all you got to do is just show up. When **Warren Buffet** was in college, he had read an item in the school newspaper according to which a $500 graduate school scholarship was to be awarded on that particular day. It also said that the applicants should go to Room 300, where they could earn a scholarship to the accredited school of the student's choice. Buffet quickly went to Room 300, without saying anything to anyone. He was the only guy who showed up. There were 3 professors in the room who wanted to wait for other students to show up and then decide whom to give the scholarship. But Buffet quickly said, "No, no. It is now three o'clock" pointing to them that they should award the scholarship to him only. So, he won the scholarship just by being quick-witted.

. . .

If you are experienced, trust your instincts and take quick action

Richard Branson was impulsive and didn't always trust numbers. He used to make up his mind about a business proposal within just thirty seconds based on whether it excites him or not. He relied more on gut instinct than researching huge amounts of twisted statistics that at times didn't prove anything. This doesn't mean that Branson just gambles with his business plans. The efficient gut feeling develops only after one has a great experience gained through learning from failing many times at something and Branson, throughout his life has loved failing, and then learning from it, as much as he loves tasting the fruits of success.

It is far better if you can play with numbers too

However, **John D Rockefeller** was good with numbers, and calculated each risk to make the new business ideas more feasible. He would then act quickly and boldly to see it through to fruition. He was noted as staying in his office for hours, using a chalkboard which was filled with different plans and strategies to make sure his every penny is invested properly.

Chapter Forty-Four
RESILIENCE

Although the world is full of suffering, it is full also of the overcoming of it - Helen Keller

Resilience is the capacity to recover quickly from difficulties and this is one of the most important qualities of high achievers. They are ready to embrace failure and consider it as a pebble on which they stumbled upon in their clear path towards the ultimate goal. They consider universe to be friendly with them and helpful for enabling them achieve their goals, and thus take every setback, health breakdown, being criticized, being deceived by ones they trusted as some positive signal from the universe and keep moving forward.

Resilience pushes you forward

We discussed about the kicking away of **Steve Jobs** from his own company and how he regained that back with persistence and perseverance. His setback of getting kicked out pushed him to gain more experience at other companies. This way he made Apple an even greater company in the field of software and electronics. This is what is meant by being resilient and he was so optimistic that he really proved that if we consider universe as friendly towards us, it really is.

Welcome the criticism

Zuckerberg was highly criticized over privacy allegations. Had he stayed obstinate and not give heed to public opinion, his lack of resilience would have made Facebook just a historic social networking monument. However, he understood public opinion, respected it and gave users more control over their privacy. He quickly learned how much the user experience mattered and thus, adapted his decisions to be more inclusive of them.

The women power

JK Rowling has the most powerful resilience among the top successful women of today. As discussed before, her journey from being unemployed, mother's Multiple Sclerosis and subsequent death, strained relationship with her father, divorce, insomnia, clinical depression, taking care of a small girl child, living on state benefits to becoming a multimillionaire in just five years is a clear cut example of how resilient a woman can be. Similar is the case with **Oprah Winfrey** who handled the tough situations exceptionally well.

The survival of the fittest

Resilience is all about adapting yourself to the new change and getting back stronger than before. Some high achievers have developed a mindset of everyday trying to be stronger and better than what they were yesterday. This thing takes their progress curve upward and forward always, irrespective of the tough or easy times. Even if the Darwin's theory of evolution is completely false, "the survival of fittest" fits perfect in this new generation of competition and rat race. The people who try to be better than themselves, not only separate themselves from the competition by straightaway being at the top, but they also keep evolving everyday into better and skilful humans. They never declare themselves as "broken" or "unsuccessful" until and unless they themselves feel so. The external environment literally has no effect on their internal calm and happy environment which is flooded with the visualization and "a belief that it is possible" of having a dream come true. This is what makes their life really very interesting even in the toughest times.

Chapter Forty-Five
SMART-HARD-WORK

Whenever there is a hard job to be done I assign it to a lazy man; he is sure to find an easy way of doing it - Walter Chrysler

Frankly speaking, simple hard-work today has got no value. Labourers work harder than the professionals and hardly manage their life on what they earn. Professionals work harder than their employers and those in administration and are still seemingly and comparatively underpaid. The established businessmen work less physically and just more mentally and are the highest earners in the society. So, just working hard is going to take you nowhere. You need to work hard and smart and in a proper direction towards your goals. That is going to take you somewhere successfully.

The power of intelligence
Bill Gates achieved his goals through hard work but he had a proper direction through his vision. He strongly advocates the importance of intelligence (not education). He believes that the smartness lies in knowing how to use your

intelligence, which can make you can reach your goals and targets faster and in a better way.

Be smart in innovation as well

One of the famous companies today, Apple, didn't necessarily invent things. **Steve Jobs** used the existing concepts and products and shaped them in a way that they seemed phenomenal. Same is the case with **Jeff Bezos** in case of Amazon.com. **Mark Zuckerberg** too did the same thing. Didn't the social networking sites exist before Facebook? They did, but none of the social networking site had the combined features of all those networking sites. Mark smartly stood up, combined those features, added few of his own and surprised the hard working engineers of other social networking sites.

Smartness in delegation

Richard Branson used to simply delegate tasks and be the smart boss. **Warren Buffet, Steve Jobs** and **Rockefeller** believed in hiring efficient people for the work they would delegate. They used to spend more time in hiring and finding the right talent. They believed that smartness lies in finding the people as smart as you are or smarter than you for your team. This way, if you find 9 such people and yourself also continue doing the same work, you would be increasing your productivity by 10 times.

You don't need to be Einstein or Arnold

You don't need to have an IQ that challenges Albert Einstein or strength as good as Arnold, but you need to have enough smartness to find the shortest possible way of reaching your goals, although with hard-work but the one that is less tiring. The best thing about today's entrepreneurs is that they believe in "retirement before the age of 30" and that is because of the increase in the concept of using smart hard-work instead of the life-long persistence which the entrepreneurs or successful people of the past used to have. The latter were absolutely right in their way of achieving success as they used to be their own teachers, learning from their own experience and by the time they were 40, they used to chart out a plan that they knew would succeed at.

Be smart or go home

Today is the era of internet. You can develop any skill, master any technique and have knowledge about any successful person's experience of reaching the destination that you also want to reach, thus minimize the unnecessary effort required in gaining experience from failing again and again at something. The previous era was different as there were very less educated people, lesser thinkers and even least number of people who were able to turn that idea into reality. Today, if you got an idea, and you don't patent it, by the time you would have finished developing that into the product, you would see someone already earning his/her living out of the same. Today, smartness has become a necessity. You only have two choices: either smartly work hard and you can hire people who are even smarter than you for accomplish your dreams, or you can keep working harder and harder for someone who is smarter than you and help him achieve his dreams. The choice is always yours.

Chapter Forty-Six
TAKING RISKS BUT SMARTLY

Don't be too timid and squeamish about your actions. All life is an experiment. The more experiments you make the better - Ralph Waldo Emerson

Another type of smartness that successful people believe in having is in taking risks and giant leaps. Low achievers never dare to take risks. Even if they finally take it, it would be something like gamble. This is because either they did spend too much of their time thinking whether or not to take the risk or they just took the risk blindly. Either way, they get no special advantage of taking those risks.

Highly productive, easily reversible

One good way of taking risks is taking only "those risks" which give you high productivity if you succeed, which can be reversed if they don't seem to work and do not give you much loss in case they prove worthless. **Zuckerberg** took risks from the privacy fiasco to the newsfeed, and he often had to backtrack on the changes that did not work. Still, it did not dampen his appetite for innovation.

. . .

Prediction and far-sightedness

Warren Buffett acts smartly and intelligently when it comes to taking risks. He looks for businesses in which he can predict what they're going to look like in 10 or 15 or 20 years. He just gives it a nod if he predicts that the businesses would be larger and doing more trading internationally. The exciting point about his risk taking behavior is that he doesn't call it "risk". He calls it research and believes that risk comes from not knowing what you are doing.

Protecting the downside

Branson relies on his gut feeling and experience and quickly takes risks in business. He believes that the brave may not live forever, but the cautious do not live at all. He remains prepared to get knocked down and knows that he may fail. But there is no such thing as a total failure, is there? He also firmly believes in "protecting the downside." This is another important characteristic feature of high achievers. They work out in advance all the things that could go wrong. Then they make sure they have all those eventualities covered.

The greatest risk in life

The successful people are typically not blind to risk. Nevertheless, they tend to view the seemingly "risky situations" as opportunities to be exploited. **Oprah Winfrey** believes that the success lies in stepping out of the comfort zone and taking risks. She also believes that one of life's greatest risks (and in fact the worst of all risks) is never daring to risk.

Chapter Forty-Seven
UNSELFCONSCIOUS

You wouldn't worry so much about what others think of you if you realized how seldom they do - Eleanor Roosevelt

There is a fascinating trait of most of the successful people. They don't think it to be of their business what others think of them. In fact, they don't even bother to listen to others' opinion about them unless and until it is something related to enhancement of their work. They live their personal lives the way they want, the way it seems less time consuming and the way it gives them more balance in life.

I don't care

Take the case of **Steve Jobs**, a great personality, but for the past decade almost always wore the same outfit: a black St. Croix mock turtleneck sweater, blue Levi's 501 jeans, and New Balance 991 trainers. Although he never spoke publicly about his choice of clothing, he is reported to have told his friends that he least cared about his appearance.

. . .

I have other important decisions to make

The President of USA, **Barack Obama** doesn't want to waste his energy on decision-making process about what to wear. He always wears a grey or a blue suit because he doesn't want to waste decision-making energy on what to wear. He believes that he has other important decisions to make and doesn't want to waste energy on "not so important" stuff.

That grey t-shirt on every occasion

Same is the case with **Mark Zuckerberg**. He has a set of grey t-shirts which he virtually wears on every occasion. He also believes not to waste energy on deciding what to wear and how to look good. His main focus is on his work. His main concern is how Facebook appears in front of people. He believes that people recognize you by the efficiency and productivity of your work and not by the physical appearance and clothes you wear (unless you are a movie star or a super-model)

First get to that level and then think about the edge

When you have a set routine for what you like to eat, what you wear, and how you handle other tasks of your day, this would be an amazing time-saver. It would let you focus on the really important decisions. When these great people don't care about what others would think of them, why should you? Of course having a good personality and attractiveness is good in giving you an edge over the "others", but what really matters first is reaching that level where you would be standing shoulder to shoulder with those successful "others".

Chapter Forty-Eight
VALIANT

Cowards die many times before their deaths; the valiant never taste of death but once - William Shakespeare

Valiant are the ones who show courage or determination. This is one of the characteristic traits of high achievers. They don't need courage to fight with someone or apply any physical force, but to withstand those early struggles in life, sustain those moments of failing and simultaneously keep learning from them, keep moving forward even when the situations are totally against them and for keeping motivation alive in their hearts as well as in the hearts of their teammates.

The real problem

Henry ford was a valiant person and used to advise his employees to have valiance in their hearts. He believed in finding solutions for the problems and condemned the act of wasting time and energy going around problems than in trying to solve them. The problem itself is not a problem; our timid behavior towards the problem is the actual problem.

. . .

Big problems as just a bunch of little problems

Henry Ford also gave a sure shot way of solving bigger problems with courage and determination. He advocated dividing any damn problem into small tasks, then working out the solution to the first task. This way, slowly and gradually, the whole problem gets solved without much stressing out as well. He called these big problems as just a bunch of little problems. When someone makes his/her mind to climb a mountain, even if he/she has a heart filled with immense amount of courage, he/she is going to feel a bit nervous. However, if he/she takes just one step at a time with faith, this step automatically pushes him/her forward towards the next step and so on. So, individual steps involved in climbing a mountain are not that hard, what is actually hard and important is being consistent.

Play life like a videogame

Then, there is the issue of being valiant if you fail. If you give a deaf ear to what people say about you and your failure, you could perceive your failure in a positive way. You would think of it as an opportunity to master the skill that is required in going through that step which you previously couldn't. This would help you in going through that step again in case somehow you fall from the top. You might have played that video game in your childhood which had many levels and you couldn't make through, suppose level 8. You start again and this time you try not to make that mistake again which you made previously and reach level 9. Suppose you can't clear level 10 now and have to start again from level 1, would you now make that mistake again at level 8 which you did the very first time? Absolutely no, because you have mastered that step due to your failing once, twice or as many times plus your main focus is now on clearing level 10. The same is true with the real life.

The difference lies in perception

The only difference between the timid and the valiant folks is that when the former ones fail, they consider themselves weak and unable to do the task, while the latter folks take it as a challenge, a lesson to learn from and an opportunity to master the task. They courageously take it as a reply of the universe (which they consider friendly towards them) that some skill is missing or some effort is lacking somewhere and they set up to face the situation boldly. **JK Rowling** once said: "Failure gave me an inner security that I have never had by passing examinations."

Learning lessons from failure

Even **Bill Gates,** one of the most successful persons in history feels that celebrating success was fine but what is more important than it is to heed the lessons of failure. If you don't take lessons from your mistakes, you are doomed to repeat the same mistakes. If you repeat doing the same thing over and over again, you can't expect new results. So, be valiant, learn from your mistakes, feel the fear of the situation and still do it anyway.

Chapter Forty-Nine
WILL POWER

Strength does not come from physical capacity; it comes from indomitable will - Mahatma Gandhi

The power of will is our mental faculty by which we decide on and initiate action. It all starts by taking action; the thoughts or ideas alone aren't enough. People with strong power of will, take a decision firmly and turn their ideas and plans into reality. They know how to and by when they need to execute their plans. They write their own story of success and create history by using this power.

Will power fights dyslexia

Steve Jobs believed that any person can succeed in any damn thing he/she sets his/her mind to. Successful people aren't more advantaged or more educated, they are just the ones who are willing to go out there and do it. From being a dyslexic kid who performed badly in school, **Richard Branson** went to become a British business magnate with a net worth of over 4.7 billion through his strong power of will. Having a poor academic performance due to his dyslexia, he focused more on his business which included raising parakeets and growing more and more Christmas trees. If he had not used this mental faculty, and remained a dumb person because of his dyslexia, we would not be having any Virgin today (Virgin is his billion dollar company, don't take it otherwise).

Don't worry if they call you an obstinate

Battling the depression and other social and monetary issues by a strong will power of **JK Rowling** gave us the Harry Potter. As discussed before, **Henry Ford** would take a decision and make sure that his plan works out by hook or by crook. He was called obstinate for his peak level of willpower and stick-to-it type of decision making process.

I want it and I will have it

Ford had made up his mind to build an engine with 8 cylinder cast in just one block and he instructed his engineers to produce a design for it. This would have lessened the space required for placing the engine in the motor car and thus produce a better and less spacious engine. His engineers declared that it was impossible to build such an engine. Ford commanded them to produce it any damn way. They tried and tried for 6 months but all in vain. They came back to Ford and again said that it was an impossible feat. They tried it for another six months as Ford was not ready to hear "No" from them. They still failed. At the end of the year, they again told Ford that it was impossible for them or anyone to build such an engine. Ford said to them with sheer determination: "Go right ahead. I want it and I will have it". They went ahead and succeeded this time to produce the famous V-8 motor of Ford.

. . .

I can and I will

The successful people always keep affirming different versions of the words "I can and I will". Every time they say I will, it leads to a creation, first in their minds and then in the reality. They know that the commitment and determination to execute a task is the first and most important in getting the task done than having so many skills and knowledge about how to do a task. Use your willpower, be the doer, have persistence and see how anything previously impossible becomes possible.

Chapter Fifty
XCELLENCE

If a man is called to be a street sweeper, he should sweep streets even as a Michaelangelo painted, or Beethoven composed music or Shakespeare wrote poetry. He should sweep streets so well that all the hosts of heaven and earth will pause to say, 'Here lived a great street sweeper who did his job well - Martin Luther King Jr.

You don't need to know how to swim if you are an excellent tree climber. Similarly, the intelligence of a dolphin cannot be judged on the basis of its inability to climb a tree. Your quality of being outstanding or extremely good in your own field makes you successful in that field. You don't need to know everything about everything. But if you do, that is an added advantage. The best thing about high achievers is that they either work for achieving excellence in their respective fields or they are excellent, that is why they are in that particular field.

Excellence is cultivable

Before achieving success, almost all successful people knew they were going to do it, but very few among them knew how they were going to do it. So, the excellence is cultivable. It is just a baby of repetition. As **Aristotle** said, "We are what we repeatedly do. Excellence, then, is not an act, but a habit."

Excellence in earning money

Rockefeller learnt how to always get the best deal in all things from his father. He got a lesson on persistence from his struggling mother. He finally cultivated excellence from his own experience of small businesses he involved himself into and became the world's first billionaire and the richest American in history. He had developed such perfection in calculation and dealing with numbers that he's counting his total worth dollar after dollar would take months.

Excellence in his own work

Del Vecchio developed excellence for making eye glasses by working in a factory that made molds for auto parts and eyeglass frames. He even lost part of his finger during an accident over there. Then, at the age of 23, he opened his first molding shop called Luxottica which expanded to be the world's largest maker of sunglasses and prescription eyeglasses. Today, Luxottica, the known maker of Oakley eyewear and Ray-Ban, also owns 6,000 Sunglass Hut and Lenscrafters retail shops. He is among the top richest man in Italy just because of his excellence in his own field.

Excellence in managing time

Henry ford mastered his time and was an excellent time manager. He believed that most people get ahead during the time that others waste. He also excelled in the process of thinking productively which gave him an edge over the other entrepreneurs of his time. He knew that thinking was one of the hardest works, and used to spend time fruitfully in thinking how to be more productive and how to make better plans. His curious mind regarding the automobiles and machines also fetched him great success.

Major in major things

However, many people start getting excellent in those areas which would prove less productive to them. **Tony Robbins** attributes the failure of those people to "Majoring" in minor things while they should have been doing the reverse. You should give your attention and time to what matters the most for you. When you dedicate your life to doing only big things, the little things can be taken care of by someone else for you. In short, you need to Major in major things and that would prove fruitful in the long run.

Chapter Fifty-One

HAVING A YOUTHFUL MIND AT EVERY AGE

Everyone is the age of their heart - Guatemalan Proverb

As you keep getting closer and closer towards your deathbed, your physical body ages, so does your mind. However, there are people who keep their minds young by the power of affirmations. No doubt, with ageing, you get to have more and more experience and maturity; however that freshness of ideas and that creativity starts losing from your minds. High achievers keep their thinking young at all ages because they know the essence of being young and energetic and it just becomes their habit to think like a hypothetical person who is in his 20's and has as much experience as they have in their 40's or 50's. They get a double advantage just by a slight change in perception on a constant basis.

The secret code of Steve Jobs

Steve Jobs is the best example of a successful person who maintained a youthful mind and used to reveal this secret in a secret message. He always used to say: "Stay hungry. Stay foolish" What he meant by staying hungry is that successful people have a drive that keeps them coming back for more. They are hungry for more instead of thinking that what they have is sufficient for the long term. This is different from greed or being ungrateful as this hunger acts as a motivational force which drags them along the path from achieving one goal to achieving a bigger one and so on. If you lose this hunger, your era ends, you lose this passion and your game is over. This is one of the attributes of a youthful mind and this process of staying hungry ends by the time you cross your 50's. Jobs was a man of his words. If he advised people to stay hungry, he followed it as well. He attended the meetings or product launches of Apple even when he was so weak and old and too ill with cancer.

Now let's analyse how staying foolish would keep us young. By "stay foolish" he meant that we should challenge the basic assumptions which are accepted by the society and other people without questioning. You would seem foolish to the society by asking why something should be done the way it is done, or by following such an untrodden path which you know would be productive but "they" never tried. This is what a child does by sometimes asking those questions which even adults can't answer. So, it is a natural trait in a human being of being curious, take risks, follow a path full of adventure and this trait is unfortunately called "foolishness" as we grow old. So, staying foolish helps and you make mistakes, not caring about what others say and just gaining experience and carving out a path for you and for "others" to follow (whose parents or grandparents considered you foolish once).

The part of his game

Warren Buffet claims that he makes plenty of mistakes and that he'll make plenty more mistakes, too. This is the part of his game. He just makes sure that the right things overcome the wrong ones. When you fall down from the ladder 10 times, 11th time you are surely going to climb it if you kept learning all those 10 times.

Never give 100% perfect review

Richard Branson also feels that being young in the mind at all ages is what helps in getting success over others. He just simplifies the secret code of Steve Jobs in comprehendible words. He believes that there's such an inherent danger in letting people think that they have perfected something and tend to sit back and rest on their laurels while countless others will be labouring furiously to better their work. This is the reason he never gives anyone a 100% perfect review of their work. He thinks that no matter how "brilliantly conceived" something is, there always remains a little room for improvement.

Never settle down as you are not mud

Rockefeller never settled and was not afraid to give up the good to go for the great. He is still a prime example of someone who went for the great. Whenever he decided to take over any business, he would employ his ruthless tactics. After making an above-the-market-value offer to the company in hopes the company would sell. If they didn't want to take that generous offer, then he would literally drive them out of the competition. Simply put, he never settled, growing his companies, keeping strategizing and executing new ways to grow his net worth.

Chapter Fifty-Two
ZEALOUS

Zeal is a volcano, the peak of which the grass of indecisiveness does not grow - Khalil Gibran

High achievers have a great amount of zeal in them. The show great energy or enthusiasm in their pursuit of a cause or an objective. They have already visualized their success and thus, they believe that it can happen and are determined that it will happen. This thing provides them an unprecedented surge of motivation which makes them work harder and harder in the pursuit of their goal. The difference between their hard-work and the hard-work of the low achievers is that the latter work with lack of energy or enthusiasm while the former don't take any action by unwillingness. In fact their action taking process has been given a name "inspired action" which is very less tiring and they even don't feel like they were working until they achieve what they aspire for.

He sold ties to his classmates and they still buy them from him

Ralph Lauren was born in a strict Jewish family. His

father was a house painter, but Ralph still had big dreams. He was very enthusiastic for becoming a millionaire, and had mentioned this thing in his yearbook as well. He started very early with selling ties to his classmates to earn some cash. His interest in ties and his zealous nature for becoming a millionaire helped him put his foot through the door of bigger achievements in the clothing industry. In 1974, he was signed on to design the clothes for 'The Great Gatsby' in 1974. Then he was pushed into so much of fame with his name being one of the top clothing brands in the world.

Passion has energy

Oprah Winfrey's zealous mentality helped her go from hosting a talk show to becoming one of the richest women in the world. Zealous and over-achieving entrepreneurs like Oprah tend to have a very strong desire to attain very high milestones. They want to be the best at what they do. These successful people are willing to make some sort of sacrifice to get ahead in order to get their desired goal. Oprah believes that passion has energy and we need to feel the power that comes from doing whatever excites us.

Focus brings enthusiasm

According to **Tony Robbins**, our energy and enthusiasm is dependent on our focus. Where the focus goes, energy flows. What we focus on is the thing that feels real to us in the moment. Also, whatever we pay more attention to in our lives, we tend to grow that and move towards that. If we are focused on how we can add more value to our business or organization, we will consistently and enthusiastically find ways to add more of those values. If we shift our focus on the excuses for why we can't achieve something, we will be empowering more and more of that limiting belief.

Be results-focussed rather than activity-focussed

The other great advice by **Tony Robbins** regarding the beautiful interaction of zeal and focus is that we should be results-focused rather than activity-focused. When we know the result we are after, we are more likely to come up with greater actions to take us more efficiently, effectively and rapidly towards those the attainment of those results.

He doesn't stop writing and thus remains zealous and famous

James Patterson is the top international bestselling author. He feels that one of his success secrets is he never stops writing. He is so much passionate and enthusiastic about writing that if he hits a block on one story, he works on another. He even claims to work on writing about 20 stories at a time and if he can't think for any of them, he just starts a new one to do. Whether it's a science fiction, mystery, or something for teens, he keeps on writing. This sort of overproduction of books helps him be fresh in the minds of people and maintain his zealous nature.

AFTERWORD

The final point about the qualities of all the successful people who walked on the surface of earth during 20th and 21st centuries is the concept of self-control. The most important thing about all these qualities is that you cannot instil them in your life until you have such a powerful inner magnet that directs the compass of your life, until you are the captain of your own ship or the pilot of your own life. By practicing the qualities, habits, methods, ideas, and techniques in this book, you will become a master of your own personal and professional success, and inspire others who come along or who have similar goals and vision as yours. One of the purposes of life is to learn and teach others what you learn and believe is true. Let us together join hands to be the change we want to see in the world. Let us pledge together that we will achieve our highest potentials in any field we are, render our services to humanity in any way we can and enhance and improve the overall quality of the short human life on earth.

Thank you and we wish you all the best in using these qualities in every part of your life.

Best regards,
Matt Morris, CPCC and Dr. Shah Faisal Ahmad